THE
BOYS
NEXT
DOOR

A
SCREENPLAY

BY ANTHONY REYES

FADE IN:

EXT. MONTANORO HOME - DAY

A moving truck pulls up into the driveway of a beautiful suburban house. A car pulls up behind the truck, and JOHN and NANCY MONTANORO step out of the car.

The rear doors open, and the Montanoro twins, JULIAN and JASON, get out. Both are 17, good looking, and in physically good shape.

Julian looks around in disgust as he sees:

White picket fences.

Perfect lawns.

Beautiful houses.

JULIAN
I think I just threw up in my mouth.

JASON
What's up?

JULIAN
What is this? Wisteria Lane?

John turns to Julian.

JOHN
If you don't like the neighborhood, you can always move.

Julian gives John a dirty look as John walks over to the moving truck to help the movers. The boys continue to stake out the neighborhood until they spot ADAM and AMANDA CLARK across the street.

EXT. CLARK HOME/FRONT YARD - DAY

Amanda sits on the steps of her front porch surfing the net. She stops and looks at Julian. Her brother, Adam, is shooting hoops in the driveway. He stops dribbling the ball and looks across the street.

EXT. CLARK HOME/FRONT YARD - DAY

CASSANDRA "KIKI" SINCLAIR walks down the street talking on her cell phone. She stops and watches the movers across the street moving furniture into the Montanoro house.

EXT. CLARK HOME/FRONT YARD - DAY

Amanda walks over to Kiki.

> KIKI
> Oh, come on, Kev. Why are you giving me shit? I told you, she has no idea what's going on—

Amanda taps her on the shoulder. Kiki jumps.

> KIKI (CONTINUING)
> I have to go. There's a bee buzzing. I'll call you later.

She hangs up.

> AMANDA
> What was that all about?

> KIKI
> Oh, it was nothing. Just Sophie. Rick gave her chlamydia again.

> AMANDA
> Ewwww…

Kiki points at Julian and Jason.

> KIKI
> Who are they?

                              AMANDA
        I don't know.

Adam appears.

                              ADAM
        There's finally a family moving in. That place has
        been empty for months.

EXT. MONTANORO HOME/DRIVEWAY - DAY

Julian and Jason lean against the car with their arms crossed.
They stare at the trio.

EXT. CLARK HOME/FRONT YARD - DAY

                              ADAM
        Hey, are they twins?

                              KIKI
        Is your brain leaking? What do you think, genius?

                              AMANDA
        Let's go meet them.

                              ADAM
        Sure.

The trio crosses the street. Kiki stops and pulls Adam to the side.

                           KIKI
          I have first dibs. I saw them first, bitch.

EXT. MONTANORO HOME/DRIVEWAY - DAY

Jason grabs Julian's hand.

                           JASON
          OMG! They're crossing the street.

                           NANCY
          Who?

                           JULIAN
          The people across the street, that's who.
                (beat)
          Jason, please let go of my hand.

Jason lets go.

                           JOHN
          I'm going inside.

                           NANCY
          John, don't you want to meet the new neighbors?

                           JOHN
          No.

Amanda, Adam, and Kiki approach the twins.

AMANDA
Hi, I'm Amanda—

KIKI
Hi, I'm Cassandra Sinclair, but everyone calls me
Kiki.

Julian, ignoring Kiki, extends his hand to Amanda.

JULIAN
Hi, I'm Julian. This is my brother, Jason.

Jason waves.

AMANDA
Nice to meet you. This is my brother, Adam.

ADAM
Hey, how's it going?

He shakes Julian's and Jason's hands.

JASON
You've got a pretty strong grip there, my friend.

JULIAN
(under his breath)
I bet he does.

Amanda smiles at John. He stands in the middle of the driveway staring at them. She waves at him. He rolls his eyes at her, takes a box from one of the movers, and enters the house.

> KIKI
> I'm Kiki, but I'm sure you already know that.

> JULIAN
> Yeah, I heard you the first time, Cassandra.

> NANCY
> Guys, your father and I will be inside helping the movers.

> JULIAN
> We'll be out here.

John saunters out of the house.

> JOHN
> We could use some help over here.

> JULIAN
> That's what Pedro and Pico are for.

> KIKI
> (laughing)
> You're sassy. I love it. You have to come to my party tonight.

NANCY

Jason, most of these boxes over here are yours.
C'mon, please take them inside.

Julian gestures for Jason to do what he's told. Jason sucks his teeth
and looks over to Adam.

JASON

Would you mind helping me?

Adam looks over to his sister. She nods in approval.

ADAM

Sure.

Adam and Jason each pick up a box, and they enter the house.

JULIAN

So, Amanda, I take it that you live across the street?

AMANDA

I do—

KIKI

I don't live too far from here, either.

JULIAN

(to Amanda)
Cool. At least now I have someone around here that
I can call a friend.

Amanda smiles at him.

                    KIKI
    I'm just as friendly.

Julian continues to ignore Kiki.

                    AMANDA
    You know, if you need someone to show you around,
    just let me know.

                    JULIAN
    Yeah, that would be cool.

Kiki's cell rings.

                    KIKI
    Oh shit, I have to take this. I'll be right back.

                    JULIAN
    Take your time.

Amanda turns away, holding back her laughter.

                    JULIAN (CONTINUING)
    What?

                    AMANDA
    You're too funny.

JULIAN

I'm considered to be many things.

AMANDA

Is that so?

JULIAN

Oh, yeah. By the way, what are you doing tonight?
Wanna hang?

Amanda looks at him for a moment and smiles.

AMANDA

Nine o'clock work for you?

JULIAN

Sounds like a plan.

Kiki appears.

KIKI

Where is your brother? He's been gone, like, forever.

Jason and Adam walk out of the house. Adam approaches his
sister with a flustered look on his face. His shirt is partially
untucked.

ADAM

Are you ready to go?

                    AMANDA
Yeah.

                    JULIAN
See you tonight, Amanda.

                    KIKI
          (whispering to Amanda)
You're seeing him tonight? You're such a slut.

                    AMANDA
Giving up your title so soon?

                    KIKI
Anyway, it was nice meeting you, Julian. Hopefully
I'll see you around. It was nice meeting you too,
whatever your name is.

                    JASON
It's Jason, sweetheart.

Jason turns to Adam.

                    JASON (CONTINUING)
Nice meeting you, Adam.

                    ADAM
          (awkward)
Yeah. Cool.

Kiki and Amanda cross the street. Amanda turns and smiles at Julian.

> ADAM (CONTINUING)
> OK, see you guys around.

Jason shakes Adam's hand and looks him over.

> JULIAN
> You two make a cute couple.

Jason gives Julian a stern look.

> JASON
> Don't go there.

> JULIAN
> (to Adam)
> I say go for it, studly. If my brother is anything like me, you're going to have your hands full, or not.

Julian smiles at Adam and goes into the house.

> ADAM
> Your brother's an asshole.

Adam walks across the street.

> JASON
> (to himself)
> Yes, my brother *is* an asshole.

Jason goes into the house.

INT. CLARK HOME/LIVING ROOM - DAY

Adam sits down on the sofa, turns on the television, and spaces out.

> AMANDA (O.S.)
> Hey, are you OK?

> ADAM
> (startled)
> Hey, what's up? How long have you been there?

> AMANDA
> Long enough to see you spacing out.

She sits next to him.

> AMANDA (CONTINUING)
> So, what did you think of them?

> ADAM
> They're OK.

> AMANDA
> They're hot. I mean, like, really hot.

> ADAM
> Relax, girl. If I had to choose, I'd say that Jason's the one with all the charm.

                    AMANDA
No, Julian's the one with the charm.

                    ADAM
I don't think so.

                    AMANDA
I'm hanging with him tonight. Do you want to come
with?

                    ADAM
Nah, I'm staying home.

                    AMANDA
With Dad? You can't keep babysitting him every
weekend. Where is he?

                    ADAM
Upstairs. Hung over.

They sit quietly as Adam takes the remote and cable surfs.

                    ADAM (CONTINUING)
By the way, Julian totally outed me.

                    AMANDA
Totally?

                    ADAM
Totally.

INT. MONTANORO HOME/JULIAN'S BEDROOM - NIGHT

Julian unpacks his boxes of clothes.

He begins to put them in the closet.

Jason lies on Julian's bed throwing a ball back and forth against the wall.

JULIAN
Would you stop that? It's annoying me.

Jason stops.

He throws the ball out the window.

JASON
Happy now?

JULIAN
Very much, thank you. What's your problem?

JASON
Why did you have to be such a dick to him?

JULIAN
Because I wanted to.

JASON
I'm serious.

JULIAN

Me too.

JASON

Don't fuck this up for me, Julian. I like him.

JULIAN

Already? Here we go again.

JASON

What do you mean by that?

JULIAN

We both know what happened to the last guy you
had a crush on.

JASON

Why are you bringing him up?

JULIAN

Only to remind you that it's best to take things one
step at a time. Why can't you get your shit together?

JASON

It's just that…

JULIAN

It's just what?

JASON

It's just that I could never understand how people
automatically gravitate toward you, and I get treated
like the redheaded, freckled stepchild.

JULIAN

Maybe, it's because you act like the redheaded,
freckled stepchild, or maybe it's because you're
needy and insecure. If I had to pick, I'd say you're
needy.

JASON

You know what I'm saying is true. You've always
been everyone's favorite.

JULIAN

True, but maybe it's because I'm not needy and
insecure.

There is a knock on the door. Julian opens the door to see Nancy
standing in the hallway holding a takeout menu.

NANCY

Hey, I was going to order takeout for our first night.
What do you think?

JULIAN

I think you should acquire culinary skills. It's no
wonder your husband has high cholesterol. Try
cooking a meal for once.

Julian leaves the bedroom.

                    JULIAN (O.S.) (CONTINUING)
          I'm going to take a shower.

Jason takes the menu from Nancy.

                    JASON
          I'll take a look and get back to you.

Jason shuts the door in her face.

INT. MONTANORO HOME/BATHROOM - NIGHT

Julian turns on the light and closes the door.

He takes off his shirt and turns the shower on.

He stares at himself in the mirror.

His eyes start to tear up.

A tear rolls down his face as the steam from the shower fogs up
the mirror.

FADE TO BLACK:

INT. CLARK HOME/FRONT DOOR - NIGHT

There is a knock, and PETER CLARK opens the door. Julian
stands in the doorway.

JULIAN

Hello, I'm here to pick up Amanda.

PETER

And your name is…?

JULIAN

I'm Julian Montanoro. My family and I just moved in across the street.

PETER

Come in.

Julian enters.

PETER (CONTINUING)

I saw the moving truck earlier today. I'm Peter Clark, Amanda's father.

JULIAN

Nice to meet you.

PETER

You know, actually, your name does sound familiar. You have a brother? Jason, is it?

JULIAN

Word spreads around here quickly. Remind me to lower the shades at night.

PETER

I spoke to your mother on several occasions
before you moved into the neighborhood; that's
how I know. She wanted to know more about
the high school. I guess she decided to continue
homeschooling you.

There's an uncomfortable silence.

PETER (CONTINUING)

I'm the principal.

Amanda walks down the stairs.

AMANDA

Hi, Julian.

JULIAN

(ignoring Peter)
Hey, there.

AMANDA

Are you ready?

PETER

Where are you headed tonight?

AMANDA

I'm taking Julian to Kiki's party.

PETER
OK, but I don't want you staying out too late.

Adam walks down the stairs.

JULIAN
Hey, Adam, how are you?

ADAM
Good, thanks.

AMANDA
Dad, where are your car keys?

PETER
In my office. I'll go get them for you.

Amanda follows her father, leaving Julian and Adam alone.

JULIAN
I thought you were studying tonight.

ADAM
I did, I was.

JULIAN
Which is it?

Adam doesn't respond.

> JULIAN (CONTINUING)
> My brother's home, if you're interested.

> ADAM
> No, thanks.

> JULIAN
> Just so you know, my brother is crushing on you. I'm talking, like, stalker crushing.

Adam doesn't respond.

> JULIAN (CONTINUING)
> I'm just fucking with you. He is crushing on you, though.

Adam remains silent.

> JULIAN (CONTINUING)
> I can understand why you wouldn't pursue him. It must be really hard to live in a society that judges your lifestyle. How do you cope?

> ADAM
> Excuse me?

> JULIAN
> There's nothing to be ashamed of, Adam. Just be yourself.

ADAM

I'm not ashamed of anything—

JULIAN

You don't have to explain. Coming out is a personal
decision.

AMANDA (O.S.)

Are you ready?

Julian turns to Amanda.

JULIAN

Yup.

Peter enters.

PETER

I don't want you home too late.

AMANDA

Dad, you're like a dog with a bone. Let it go, already.

JULIAN

Are you ready?

AMANDA

Let's go.

                    JULIAN
It was good seeing you again, Adam. Don't worry.
You're going to be just fine.

Julian smiles at Peter, grabs Amanda by the hand, and ushers her
out the door.

EXT. CLARK HOME - NIGHT

Julian kisses Amanda on the lips. She stops short and turns away.

                    AMANDA
    I can't.

                    JULIAN
    Yes, you can.

                    AMANDA
    No, really, I can't. I have a boyfriend. Well, sort of.

                    JULIAN
    Sort of?

He kisses her again.

Both are unaware that Peter is looking at them from the living-
room window.

She stops short again.

                    AMANDA
    I think we should get going.

                    JULIAN
        OK.

Julian and Amanda get in the car and drive off.

INT. MONTANORO HOME/LIVING ROOM - NIGHT

John is sitting in front of the fireplace and staring at the flames.

Nancy walks in holding a box. She places it down and begins to
unpack it. She has a sad look on her face.

                    JOHN
    What's wrong?

                    NANCY
    No matter how much I try, I know that they hate me.

                    JOHN
    What happened?

                    NANCY
    Julian can't stand being in the same room with me,
    and Jason walks by me like I don't even exist. It
    hurts.

She takes out a photo of Julian and Jason and places it on the
mantel above the fireplace.

                    NANCY (CONTINUING)
          It happened three years ago today. That night
          changed everything.

She takes out another photo and places it next to the picture of
Julian and Jason. It's a photo of their triplet brother JAMES.

                    JOHN
          That night didn't change anything. They were always
          this way.
               (beat)
          What are you doing?

                    NANCY
          He was our son too.

Nancy continues to unpack the box and places another photo on
the mantel.

                    NANCY (CONTINUING)
          Where did we go wrong, John?

                    JOHN
          We? Where did you go wrong? That's what you
          should be asking yourself. Do you want to cause
          problems around here? You know how they feel
          about us displaying James's picture.

NANCY

What am I supposed to do? Ignore the fact that
we had another son? And don't give me that *you*
bullshit. We're both just as guilty.

JOHN

You don't have to remind me of what I'm guilty of.
I live with it every day of my life. Speak and see no
evil, right?

Nancy stops unpacking, goes over to John, and embraces him.

JOHN (CONTINUING)

I can't live like this, Nancy.

He kisses her on the forehead.

JOHN (CONTINUING)

Just try not to make waves, OK?

NANCY

How am I making waves?

JOHN

Because you know how they feel about him.

JASON (O.S.)

Feel about what?

John and Nancy turn to Jason's voice.

                    JASON (CONTINUING)
        Feel about what, Dad?

Jason looks over to the mantel and removes James's picture. He
looks it over and throws the picture into the fireplace.

He turns to Nancy.

                    JASON (CONTINUING)
        Are you ordering takeout, or what? I'm famished.

                    NANCY
        I could order Chinese if you want.

                    JASON
        Perfect. I'd like an order of orange chicken with brown
        rice, and a side order of vegetable steam dumplings.

                    NANCY
        OK.

                    JASON
        I'll be up in my room unpacking if you need me, Nancy.

Jason leaves the living room.

Nancy looks at John with a look of despair.

EXT. KIKI'S HOME - NIGHT

Julian and Amanda park the car across the street.

There are TEENAGERS walking in and out of the house laughing and having a good time.

They get out of the car and walk toward the house.

> JULIAN

Wow, nice place.

> AMANDA

Every year, before spring break ends, Kiki throws a back-to-school party.

> JULIAN

Kiki's the thin, pale girl I met this morning, right?

> AMANDA

Yup. Oh, before I forget, if she looks high, it's because she is.

They reach the door.

> AMANDA (CONTINUING)

This will be fun. You'll see.

> JULIAN

Oh, yeah, I'm definitely looking forward to it.

They go into the house.

INT. KIKI'S HOME/LIVING ROOM - NIGHT

Kiki is holding and spilling her cocktail while speaking to a group of GIRLS. The group starts cackling like hyenas.

She turns and sees Amanda with Julian.

> KIKI
> Amanda, sweetie!

Kiki staggers over to them.

> KIKI (CONTINUING)
> I'm so fucked up right now.

> JULIAN
> Ya think?

> KIKI
> Amanda, where's Adam? Is he out?

> AMANDA
> That's so not funny. It's not easy for him, and I'd appreciate it if you'd stop—

> KIKI
> What are you talking about? Did Adam come out with you?

> AMANDA
> What? No, he stayed home.

                    KIKI
        (to Julian)
She really needs to remove that stick from out of her
ass.

Kiki looks over to Amanda, who is now walking toward another
FEMALE FRIEND. She sucks her teeth and turns to Julian.

                KIKI (CONTINUING)
Maybe after the party, you and I could get better
acquainted. Ya think?

                    JULIAN
I don't think that's going to happen.

                    KIKI
Why not?

                    JULIAN
I don't like you.

                    KIKI
Why is that?

                    JULIAN
Because you look haggard and frail, and you have
the sex appeal of a rabid dog. Eat something,
sweetie, eat. It'll do you some good.

Kiki is stunned.

> JULIAN (CONTINUING)
> It's good seeing you again.

He goes over to Amanda, takes her by the hand, and pushes her farther into the party.

EXT. CLARK HOME - NIGHT

The garage door opens, and Adam drags out two garbage bags. He places them into the trash can.

> PETER (O.S.)
> Adam, remember to take the garbage out.

> ADAM
> I'm doing that now.
> (whispering)
> Fuck. Get off my back.

Jason places his hand on Adam's shoulder.

> ADAM (CONTINUING)
> You scared the shit out of me! What are you doing—

Jason pushes Adam back into the garage. The garage door closes.

INT. CLARK HOME/GARAGE - NIGHT

Jason starts kissing him. Adam resists at first but returns the kiss. Adam stops and pushes Jason away.

                    JASON
Why did you stop?

                    ADAM
I can't do this.

                    JASON
What's the problem?

                    ADAM
There is no problem. It's just that…I don't know…

                    JASON
Don't worry about it. I understand; I've been there.

Jason brushes the hair from Adam's face.

                    JASON (CONTINUING)
Now, I'm not.

The lights turn on.

                    PETER
Adam, what's going on? Julian? I thought you were
with Amanda?

                    ADAM
This isn't Julian. This is his brother, Jason.

                    PETER
What were the both of you doing in here?

JASON
I thought that my brother was over here.

PETER
You thought that your brother was in the garage?

ADAM
Jason was helping me with the garbage bags. One of them broke.

Jason notices that Peter's eyes are glassy and that he is holding a glass of liquor.

PETER
No, your brother's not here.

JASON
Oh, OK. I also came over because my mom wanted me to invite you and your family over to dinner tomorrow night.

PETER
Sorry, we can't make it. Some other time.

JASON
You got it. You both have a good night. I'll see you around, Adam.

Adam opens the garage door, and Jason leaves.

                    ADAM
What are we doing tomorrow night that we can't go
over for dinner?

                    PETER
I like to keep distance. Especially when I know that
the kid who lives across the street has a thing for my
son.

Peter takes a sip from his glass.

                    PETER (CONTINUING)
Besides, I don't want the neighbors talking about
you and that kid. I'm not blind, Adam. You can at
least be discreet about it.

                    ADAM
Discretion? Really? Practice what you preach, Dad.
Maybe you should try being discreet when it comes
to your drinking.

                    PETER
What do you mean by that?

                    ADAM
Make sure the next time you crawl out of the
woodwork, you're not holding a glass of Jack
Daniel's. You don't want everyone to know what *we*
know.

Adam walks out of the garage as Peter quickly disposes of the remainder of his drink with one final swig.

INT. KIKI'S HOME/LIVING ROOM - NIGHT

Julian and Amanda hang around a group of TEENS, laughing and drinking. Julian looks over at a teenage boy, who looks his way while speaking to Kiki.

> JULIAN
> Amanda, who's the guy talking to Kiki?

> AMANDA
> Shit. His name is Kevin.

> JULIAN
> Who's he?

> AMANDA
> My boyfriend, ex-boyfriend. It's complicated.

KEVIN approaches Amanda.

> KEVIN
> Hey, what's up, girl. You haven't returned any of my calls.

Kevin moves closer to her.

> AMANDA
> That's because I don't want to talk to you.

                    KEVIN
Can we talk now?

                    AMANDA
Now's not a good time.

                    KEVIN
When is it ever a good time for you?

She backs away from him.

                    AMANDA
You've been drinking.

                    KEVIN
It's a fucking party. Lighten the fuck up.

He grabs her arm.

                    KEVIN (CONTINUING)
Let's talk, now.

                    AMANDA
I said no.
        (beat)
Kevin, let go of my arm.

Julian pushes Kevin away from Amanda.

                    JULIAN
Are you deaf? She doesn't want to talk to you.

Kevin gets up in Julian's face.

> KEVIN
> Who the fuck are you?

> JULIAN
> That's for you to find out.

Kiki gets in between Julian and Kevin.

> KIKI
> You're scaring away the guests, boys.

> AMANDA
> Come on, Julian, let's get out of here.

Julian and Amanda leave the party.

> KEVIN
> You just fucked yourself, Amanda! It's not over until I say it is!

Kiki puts her arms around Kevin's waist.

> KIKI
> Kevin, really, I don't see how you can even stand that girl.

> KEVIN
> Please, go eat something. Really, you look like shit.

EXT. KIKI'S HOME - NIGHT

Amanda rushes to the car.

> JULIAN
> Amanda, wait up!

> AMANDA
> I'm going to take you home.

Julian stops her.

> JULIAN
> You are not taking me back home.

> AMANDA
> Where do you want to go?

> JULIAN
> Anywhere.

They get into the car and drive off. Both of them are unaware of Kevin and the two teenage BOYS trailing in the car behind them.

INT. KIKI'S HOME/LIVING ROOM - NIGHT

Kiki pushes her way through the crowd.

> KIKI
> (to the crowd)
> Has anyone seen Kevin?

No one responds.

> KIKI (CONTINUING)
> Hello?

Someone throws a condom wrapper at her. She picks it up and throws it back.

> KIKI (CONTINUING)
> Fuck you, Rick! You should have used one on Sophie. You asshole.

She looks around the room.

> KIKI (CONTINUING)
> (to herself)
> Fuck.

Kiki storms out of the living room and out the front door.

EXT. MONTCLAIR HIGH SCHOOL/FOOTBALL FIELD - NIGHT

Amanda and Julian are sitting on the bleachers kissing. He stops.

> JULIAN
> What's up with you and Kevin?

Amanda pauses for a moment.

AMANDA

I think he's cheating on me.

JULIAN

With who?

AMANDA

I have my suspicions.

JULIAN

How long were you two together?

AMANDA

A year or so. During that time, he really helped me
deal with a lot of things.

JULIAN

Deal with what?

Amanda pauses again.

AMANDA

My mom's death.

JULIAN

Oh, I'm sorry. How did it happen?

AMANDA

She and my dad were in a car accident.

                    JULIAN
Shit, I'm sorry.

                    AMANDA
He's still not over it. I know he misses her.

There is a short silence between them.

                    AMANDA (CONTINUING)
I'm sorry. I didn't mean to make you feel
uncomfortable.

                    JULIAN
You're not making me feel uncomfortable. I know
how it feels to lose someone you really love.

                    AMANDA
Really? What happened?

                    JULIAN
There's nothing to tell.

                    AMANDA
You wouldn't have mentioned it if there was nothing
to tell.

Julian remains silent.

                    AMANDA (CONTINUING)
At least you have your brother. You and Jason seem
pretty close.

JULIAN
We may be twins, but we're not that close. Not as
close as I was with—

Amanda kisses him on the lips. They are interrupted by the
sound of someone clapping.

They see that it is Kevin and his two friends. Kevin takes a
swig from a can of beer and throws it at them. It barely misses
them.

AMANDA
Kevin, what are you doing here?

KEVIN
I hope I'm not interrupting anything.

JULIAN
I suggest you keep on walking.

KEVIN
What are you going to do if I don't?

Julian approaches Kevin.

JULIAN
(whispering into Kevin's ear)
Bash your head in.

KEVIN
Say what?

The other boys grab Julian and restrain him.

                    AMANDA
          What are you guys doing? Let him go!

Kevin punches Julian in the face.

                    AMANDA (CONTINUING)
     Stop it, Kevin!

Julian falls to the ground as Kevin continues to punch him.

                    JULIAN
          You are so dead.

                    KEVIN
          I'd like to see you try it, dick!

He punches Julian in the face again. Amanda pushes Kevin out
of the way and gets in front of Julian.

                    AMANDA
          You're going to have to go through me, Kevin.

                    KEVIN
          Get the fuck out of the way.

                    AMANDA
          No! Tell them to let him go. This is between you and
          me, not him.

She turns to Kevin's friends.

> AMANDA (CONTINUING)
> Let him go!

Kevin gestures to his friends, and they let him go.

> AMANDA (CONTINUING)
> Are you OK?

> JULIAN
> I'm fine. Take me home.

Amanda helps Julian to the car.

> KEVIN
> Come on, Amanda. We were just having some fun.

> AMANDA
> You're an asshole, Kevin.

> KEVIN
> (to Julian)
> Take care of your wounds, kid. You don't want an infection.

Julian turns to Kevin.

> JULIAN
> Don't drink and drive, Kevin. It could be hazardous to your health.

Julian takes out his iPhone and begins to text.

INT. MONTANORO HOME/JASON'S BEDROOM - NIGHT

Jason is lying on his bed. His iPhone vibrates, and he picks it up.

He reads the text.

Jason's POV - "I need you tonight. We're going hunting. Be ready by the time I get home."

He smiles and gets off the bed.

EXT. MONTCLAIR HIGH SCHOOL/FOOTBALL FIELD - NIGHT

Kevin and his two friends are laughing and drinking beer. Julian and Jason sneak up on them. Both of them are dressed in black, wearing black thermal masks and holding baseball bats.

One of the boys turns around, and Jason swings his bat, hitting him in the head.

The other boy tries to stop him but is quickly taken down by Jason's bat.

Kevin tries to run, but Julian tackles him. Julian and Jason begin kicking Kevin repeatedly in the stomach.

Julian and Jason remove their thermal masks, revealing their identities. They put their masks back on, pick up their bats, and begin pounding away.

EXT. ISOLATED ROAD - NIGHT

Kevin is seated in the driver's seat of his car. One of the boys is seated in the passenger side, and the other is seated in the back.

Julian turns on the ignition and places the gear in drive. The car speeds down the road, hits the guard rail, and crashes down into the ravine.

Julian and Jason run as they try to avoid the lights of an oncoming vehicle.

INT. MONTANORO HOME/LIVING ROOM - NIGHT

The brothers walk in on their parents lying in front of the fireplace. They sit up and look at each other quizzically as the twins throw the blood-soaked baseball bats into the fire.

INT. MONTANORO HOME/JASON'S BEDROOM - NIGHT

Jason places his iPhone on the speaker dock. He lies on his bed as the music plays. He closes his eyes.

The music stops. Jason opens his eyes to see Julian in his bedroom.

JASON

Leave it on.

JULIAN

Aren't you tired of listening to the Scissor Sisters?

JASON

You didn't need me tonight. You could have done
this all on your own.

JULIAN

So why did you help me?

JASON

Because you're my brother. What concerns you,
concerns me.

JULIAN

So why question me?

JASON

Based on the bruises on your face, it's obvious that
he did something to you. And we both know how
vain and vindictive you are.

JULIAN

No more than you.

Jason doesn't respond.

JULIAN (CONTINUING)
He was Amanda's boyfriend.

JASON
You're up to something. I can see it in your face.

Julian sits on the bed.

JULIAN
Aren't you tired of them?

JASON
Who?

JULIAN
Mom and Dad. Aren't you tired of living with them?

JASON
I'm not particularly fond of them—

JULIAN
I'm tired.

Julian leans his head on Jason's shoulder. Jason looks at his brother strangely and slowly puts his arm around him.

JASON
Talk to me. What are you thinking about?

Julian finally notices that Jason has his arm around him.

                    JULIAN
What are you doing? Get off of me.

He gets off the bed.

                    JASON
I'm here for you if you need me.

                    JULIAN
Yeah, whatever.
        (beat)
Remember to burn the clothes in the fireplace. We
don't need this coming back to bite us in the ass.

He leaves the bedroom.

INT. MONTANORO HOME/JULIAN'S BEDROOM - DAY

Julian is doing crunches on the floor. He gets up and looks at
himself in the mirror. There is a knock on the door.

                    JULIAN
        Come in.

Jason enters.

                    JULIAN (CONTINUING)
        What do you want?

                    JASON
        Amanda is downstairs.

JULIAN

Did she mention anything?

JASON

No.

There is another knock on the door, and Nancy enters the room.

JULIAN

What is it?

NANCY

Your friend Amanda is downstairs, and she's asking
a lot of questions.

JULIAN

Relax—

NANCY

I am relaxed. She's asking me about the
homeschooling thing, and I don't know what to say.

Nancy notices the bruises on Julian's face.

NANCY (CONTINUING)

Julian, what happened to your face?

JULIAN

I got into a fight with Amanda's boyfriend, but I
fixed the problem.

                    NANCY
Fixed? Julian, what did you do?

                    JULIAN
It doesn't concern you. Where is she?

                    NANCY
She's in the kitchen.

INT. MONTANORO HOME/KITCHEN - DAY

Amanda is sitting at the table. John leans against the counter drinking coffee, ignoring her.

                    AMANDA
Have you all finished unpacking?

He sighs.

                    JOHN
No.

                    AMANDA
Well, let us know—

                    JOHN
You know, there's one thing that I enjoy the most first thing in the morning, and that's drinking my first cup of coffee. Right now, I'm not enjoying it.

Julian enters.

JULIAN

Hey, Amanda, how are you?

AMANDA

I wanted to see how you were doing.

JULIAN

I'm fine.

JOHN

At least someone is.

There is a knock on the front door.

INT. MONTANORO HOME/FOYER - DAY

Nancy opens the door. It is Peter and SHERIFF NATHAN
MCFADDEN.

NANCY

Hi, can I help you?

PETER

Hi, Mrs. Montanoro. I'm Amanda's father, Peter
Clark. We've spoken on the phone several times.

NANCY

Oh, yes. How are you? Please come in.

They enter.

NANCY (CONTINUING)
By the way, Amanda is here.

AMANDA
Dad?

PETER
Amanda, we need to talk.

NANCY
Is everything OK? Why is there a police officer here?

PETER
My apologies. This is Sheriff Nathan McFadden.

NANCY
(shaking Nathan's hand)
A pleasure to meet you.
(beat)
Is there a problem?

AMANDA
Dad, what's going on?

PETER
Sweetheart, Kevin's been killed in a car accident.

AMANDA
(breaking down)
What happened?

Peter embraces Amanda.

                    JASON (O.S.)
    What's going on?

They all turn to Jason's voice as he walks down the stairs.

                    JASON (CONTINUING)
    Why is there a police officer here? Are we on *Cops*?

                    NATHAN
    Amanda, your father said you were at Cassandra
    Sinclair's party last night.

                    AMANDA
    Yeah, I was. I mean, we both were.

                    NATHAN
    We?

                    AMANDA
    Julian and me.

                    NATHAN
    So the both of you saw him yesterday? What was he
    doing?

                    AMANDA
    He was really drunk. He was with Jake Hanson and
    Rick Hyde. They were drunk too.

PETER
(to Nathan)
Do you think they could be the two unidentified
bodies?

NATHAN
Could be. Amanda, did he tell you where he was
going after the party?

AMANDA
No, but Julian and I saw them at the school football
field. They started with Julian, and all three of them
jumped him.

NATHAN
Is that true, Julian?

JULIAN
Yes.

NANCY
They beat you? Why?

JULIAN
Mom, deep breaths.

NATHAN
(to Amanda)
Was that the last time you saw them?

AMANDA

Yes. After that, I brought Julian home.

NATHAN

OK, I'm done here for now. Someone will be contacting you and Julian for a statement.

NANCY

Why would they be contacting my son? Wouldn't this be considered a statement?

JULIAN

Yeah, it's not like I'll be pressing charges anytime soon.

NATHAN

We're just trying to rule out foul play.

AMANDA

Foul play?

NATHAN

Yes. A person was spotted running from the area where the accident occurred.

AMANDA

Really? Who?

NATHAN
Cassandra Sinclair said that she saw the car go over
the guardrail. She also claims to have seen someone
run from the scene.

AMANDA
She was probably drunk, and most likely high.

NATHAN
She helped to identify the body.

JULIAN
How so?

NATHAN
When we pulled the bodies from the wreckage,
Kevin was still alive.

JULIAN
He was what?

NATHAN
He was alive. He was also mumbling something
before he died. It was hard to understand.

PETER
(speaking to Nathan)
Nate, let us know if you need anything else.

NATHAN
I will.

PETER

We're going to head back home. Amanda, lets go.
Thank you, Mrs. Montanoro.

JOHN (O.S.)

I hope you find whoever did this

They all turn to John.

John looks directly at Julian and Jason.

INT. MONTANORO HOME/JULIAN'S BEDROOM - DAY

Jason closes the door. Julian sits on his bed and looks at his brother.

JULIAN

Are you thinking what I'm thinking?

Jason nods.

JULIAN & JASON

Kiki.

There is a knock on the door, and Nancy enters.

JULIAN

What now?

NANCY

Did you two have anything to do with this?

                    JULIAN
     Do with what?

Jason looks out the window as Sheriff McFadden drives away. He watches as Peter and Amanda cross the street.

EXT. MONTANORO HOME/STREET - DAY

Peter gives Amanda a dirty look.

                    AMANDA
     What's wrong?

                    PETER
     Why didn't you tell me that Kevin and his friends
     beat up Julian?

                    AMANDA
     I didn't think it mattered.

                    PETER
     You didn't think it mattered?

They stop in front of their house.

                    AMANDA
     What's really bothering you?

                    PETER
     What's bothering me is how cold and callous your
     new friend is.

AMANDA

You're being unfair. Kevin and his friends *did* beat
him up.

PETER

Is that your response?

AMANDA

No, Dad, it hurts me. I think it's terrible what
happened to Kevin. I just think you're being way too
harsh. How did you want him to react?

PETER

Shocked and surprised, maybe? You were.

AMANDA

I agree that he could have reacted differently, but
again, he was jumped by all three of them. You can't
blame him for not being emotional.

PETER

Oh please. His mother was more emotional. And his
brother, let's not forget him—

AMANDA

You're rambling, Dad.

PETER

No, I'm not. Did you see how they looked at each
other? It's like they're hiding something. I don't want
you or your brother anywhere near them.

AMANDA

This is not about me. It's about you not liking them.

PETER

You're right. I don't like them.

AMANDA

Well, you don't have to worry about them being
around us. They're homeschooled, remember?

PETER

That's another thing: does that woman look like she
can homeschool anyone?

AMANDA

OK, I'm going inside. Call me when your space
shuttle lands.

Amanda leaves as Peter follows behind.

INT. MONTANORO HOME/JULIAN'S BEDROOM - DAY

Julian and Jason both look at each other. They turn to Nancy.

NANCY

What happened? What did he tell her?

They move in closer to her.

JASON

Mom, I'm going to need you to do me a favor.

NANCY

What kind of favor?

INT. CLARK HOME/FRONT DOOR - DAY

There is a knock on the door, and Peter opens it. It's Julian and Jason. Peter hides his drink behind his back.

PETER

Can I help you with something?

JULIAN

Hi. We're sorry to bother you, but we were just wondering…

PETER

Wondering what?

JASON

Is it too late to register for school tomorrow?

PETER

Why? I thought your mother was homeschooling the both of you.

JASON

She was, but she can't now.

PETER

Why not?

Julian and Jason move out of Peter's way. He watches as the PARAMEDICS wheel Nancy into the ambulance.

PETER (CONTINUING)
What the hell happened to your mother?

JASON
She fell down the stairs.

PETER
(turning to Jason)
How did she fall down the stairs?

JULIAN
She tripped over one of Jason's boxes.

PETER
What about your dad?

Peter sees John in back of the paramedics.

JULIAN
(yelling to his father)
It's fine, Dad! Mr. Clark is going to watch us.

PETER
I am?

JULIAN

You're the only parental figure at the moment, and you will be our principal as of tomorrow. Legally, isn't it your responsibility?

PETER

Let's not discuss legalities. Shouldn't you be more concerned about your mom?

John approaches them.

JOHN
(to Peter)
My wife's badly hurt, and I have to go with her. Can you watch the kids?

PETER
(reluctant)
Sure. Why not?

JOHN

Thanks.

John hands him a piece of paper.

JOHN (CONTINUING)
I've written down my cell number in case you need to reach me.

PETER

If by chance you are in the hospital overnight and
can't make it back in the morning, I can register
them in school.

JOHN

Oh, no, that's fine. I can fill in for Nancy while she
recovers.

JULIAN

Dad, Mom's going to need you. I think it would be
good to be around other people until Mom gets
back. What do you think, Mr. Clark?

John gives Julian a dirty look.

PETER
(to John)
I'll make the arrangements for you. Your wife needs
you right now.

JOHN

Thanks.

John gets into the ambulance, and it takes off down the street.

PETER
(hesitantly)
Do you want to wait here until your father gets
back?

                    JULIAN
No, it's OK. We'll stay at home. If we need anything,
we'll call you.

Peter nods and closes the door without responding.

INT. CLARK HOME/LIVING ROOM - DAY

Peter watches the twins cross the street from the living room
window.

Adam enters.

                    ADAM
Dad, what happened out there? What happened to
Mrs. Montanoro?

                    PETER
I don't trust those two little fuckers.

                    ADAM
Who are you talking about?

                    PETER
Who do you think I'm talking about? Adam, get
your head from out of your ass. Those kids are
trouble.

                    ADAM
Wow, you really are a mean drunk.

Adam pulls out a bottle of vodka from the liquor cabinet. He places it on the coffee table.

> ADAM (CONTINUING)
> Your dinner is ready.

Peter remains silent.

> ADAM (CONTINUING)
> Amanda and I will be eating in the kitchen.

Adam leaves.

Peter takes another swig from his drink and continues to look out the window.

INT. MONTANORO HOME/FOYER - NIGHT

Julian opens the front door.

Amanda is standing in the doorway holding two plates wrapped in aluminum foil.

> AMANDA
> I thought you and your brother might be hungry.

Julian smiles and takes the plates from her.

> JULIAN
> Thanks.

                    AMANDA
My dad tells me that you and Jason will be starting
school with us tomorrow. Is it true?

                    JULIAN
It's true.

                    AMANDA
That's great.

                    PETER (O.S.)
Amanda, what's going on over there?

Peter approaches them.

                    PETER (CONTINUING)
Did you give them the food?

                    JULIAN
She did. Thanks, I appreciate—

                    PETER
It's getting late, Amanda. Let's go; hurry up.

Amanda gives Peter a dirty look.

                    AMANDA
Can I have a minute?

                    PETER
Sixty seconds and counting.

Peter crosses the street.

Amanda turns back to Julian.

> JULIAN
>
> Can I have a kiss?

> AMANDA
>
> Do you want to give my dad a stroke?

> JULIAN
>
> Fuck yeah.

> AMANDA
>
> Enjoy your dinner, and I'll see you tomorrow.

> JOHN (O.S.)
>
> Amanda!

> AMANDA
> (yelling)
> I'm coming!

Amanda tap kisses Julian on the lips and crosses the street.

Julian closes the door.

> JASON
>
> Who was at the door?

JULIAN

Amanda. She brought us some food. I'd take
precautions before you eat it.

JASON

Why?

JULIAN

You never know if her father laced it with arsenic.

JASON

Oh, my god, like in *Flowers in the Attic*, when the
mom laced her children's doughnuts with arsenic.
Remember?

JULIAN

No. Take the food into the kitchen. I'll be right with
you.

INT. MONTANORO HOME/KITCHEN - NIGHT

Jason places the food on the table. He takes two plates from the
cabinet and drops one of them on the floor. He takes a broom
and begins to sweep up the shattered plate.

JOHN (O.S.)

Be careful; you don't want to cut yourself.

JASON

Dad? I didn't hear you come in.

John pulls a chair back and sits down at the table.

>   JASON (CONTINUING)
>   How's Mom?

>   JOHN
>   She has two broken ribs and a broken leg.

>   JULIAN (O.S.)
>   That sucks.

Julian sits down at the table.

>   JULIAN (CONTINUING)
>   I'm sure she'll be fine.

Jason places a plate of food in front of John.

>   JOHN
>   Are you really going to register tomorrow?

>   JULIAN
>   Yup. Don't worry about us. We'll be fine.

Jason hands Julian a plate of food and sits down. John sits quietly as he watches them eat.

INT. MONTANORO HOME/JULIAN'S BEDROOM - DAY

Julian suddenly wakes up from a dream. He is out of breath and sweating.

He sits at the edge of the bed, breathing heavily, and begins to cry.

EXT. MONTANORO HOME/STREET - DAY

Jason and Julian step out of the house and walk toward the Clark house with backpacks in hand.

>   JULIAN
>   Dude, you look like a train wreck.

>   JASON
>   There's nothing wrong with how I'm dressed.

>   JULIAN
>   Jason, I'm runway, and you're reality. In reality,
>   you're not the best dresser. You dig? Anyway, my
>   concern is getting to Kiki.

>   JASON
>   Don't say another word. Peter is headed our way.

Peter approaches them.

>   PETER
>   Are you two ready? How's your mother?

>   JASON
>   Not good. She has two broken ribs and a broken leg.

                    PETER
That's terrible. Where's your father?

                    JULIAN
He's at the hospital with her. He wanted me to thank
you for the beef stew you sent over yesterday.

                    PETER
It was meat loaf.

                    JASON
              (whispering to Julian)
That was meat loaf?

                    PETER
It's getting late. Let's get going.

Julian and Jason get into Peter's car.

INT. PETER'S CAR - DAY

Peter looks in the rearview mirror and sees Julian and Jason
smiling at him.

                    PETER
Do any of you want to sit up front?

                    JULIAN & JASON
No.

                              PETER
         OK, let's go.

                              JASON
         Wait a minute. What about Adam and Amanda?
         Aren't they coming too?

                              PETER
         They left earlier this morning.

All three sit in silence.

                     PETER (CONTINUING)
         Is there anything else?

                         JULIAN & JASON
         No.

                              PETER
         Great.

Peter starts the car and drives.

INT. MONTCLAIR HIGH SCHOOL/REGISTRAR'S OFFICE -
DAY

                              PETER
         Have a seat. I need you to fill out some paper work.
         One of your parents has to sign the registration
         forms. I could bring them over to your dad tonight.
         I'll have Carmen help you fill them out.

CARMEN, a heavyset Hispanic woman, approaches them.

                    CARMEN
        Hi, my name is Carmen Clotilde Sanchez Ramirez.

                    JULIAN
    What?

She hands them the forms.

                    CARMEN
        Fill these out. I'll come back to collect them when
        you're done.

She walks away.

                    JASON
            (to Julian)
        I think that Esmeralda is going to be trouble.

Julian looks through the forms. He pulls one of them out and
shows it to Jason. Jason looks it over and rolls his eyes.

                    JULIAN
        Excuse me, Ms. Clotilde Sanchez Ramirez.
            (to Jason)
        Shit, I hope I got it right.

Carmen approaches them.

CARMEN

Yes?

JULIAN

What is this?

Julian hands her the form. She looks it over and hands it back to him.

CARMEN

It's a request for records form. We need your academic records from your prior school.

JULIAN

That's not necessary. Our mother homeschooled us.

He hands the form back to her.

CARMEN

We still need you to fill out the form.

She hands the form back.

JULIAN

Excuse me, Ms. Ramirez Clotilde Sanchez—

CARMEN

Clotilde Sanchez Ramirez.

                    JULIAN
OK, whatever.
    (beat)
We won't be able to provide you the information you
need at this moment.

                    PETER (O.S.)
What's the problem?

Peter approaches Carmen.

                    CARMEN
I was just informing them that we'll need their
academic records, and they can't provide any.

                    JASON
He never said that we couldn't.

Carmen looks at Peter.

                    JASON (CONTINUING)
Besides, we have proof. Ask Mr. Clark. He spoke to
my mother regarding this issue. Tell her, Mr. Clark.

Peter pauses for a moment.

                    PETER
I did speak to your mother, and she did mention
that you were homeschooled, but she did not
provide me with any proof.

JULIAN

Why would she need to provide you with any proof?
The only reason why we're here is because she had
an accident.

PETER

True, but—

JULIAN

And as you know, Jason and I are not at the legal age
where we can make this type of decision concerning
our education without the consent of a legal
guardian or parent—

PETER

Carmen, we can hold off on the request for records
form.

Julian and Jason look at each other and exchange a silent smile.

PETER (CONTINUING)

We do, however, need you to provide us proof of
immunization. Can you at least tell us if you, or
anyone in your family, is allergic to anything so we
can inform our school nurse?

JASON

Penicillin.

Julian and Jason search their backpacks, and each pulls out a
certificate of immunization.

                    JULIAN
All you need to know is here.

They hand them to Carmen.

                    JULIAN (CONTINUING)
These are originals, and we'd like them back.

                    JASON
Yeah.

INT. HOSPITAL/NANCY'S ROOM - DAY

Nancy lies on her bed staring out the window. She looks to the
foot of the bed and stares at John as he sleeps on the visitor's
chair. John slowly opens his eyes and smiles at her.

                    JOHN
How are you feeling?

                    NANCY
You want to know how I'm feeling? My leg is killing
me, and the Vicodin hasn't kicked in. That's how I'm
feeling, John.

                    JOHN
Forget that I asked.

                    NANCY
Where's Julian and Jason?

JOHN
I had Peter Clark register them for school.

NANCY
What? Why did you let him do that? Are you
insane?

JOHN
What choice did I have, Nancy? Right now, you're
my main concern, not them.

NANCY
They can't be trusted, John. I'm scared that it's going
to happen all over again.

John leans forward and kisses her.

JOHN
We have a choice, baby. We can make this stop. We
can—

NANCY
We can't do that. I won't turn them in.

JOHN
After what they just did to you, I can't believe that
you would still protect them.

NANCY
They didn't do anything. I tripped.

                    JOHN
Tripped, or pushed?

                    NANCY
Don't do it, John. Everything will come out.
Including what happened to James.

                    JOHN
I don't care anymore. They're both out of control.
Now more than ever.

                    NANCY
I can't do it, John.

                    JOHN
That's what they're counting on. They threaten us
with their looks and without saying a word. We're
prisoners in our own home, Nance, and do you
know why?

                    NANCY
Why?

                    JOHN
Because that's how evil works.

INT. MONTCLAIR HIGH SCHOOL/JASON'S HOMEROOM -
DAY

The classroom is filled with STUDENTS talking and laughing.

Jason sits in the back of the classroom with his arms crossed.

The homeroom teacher, MARK BLANK, enters the room.

> MR. BLANK
> OK, everyone settle down.

The students continue speaking to one another.

> MR. BLANK (CONTINUING)
> I said settle down!

The students quiet down.

> MR. BLANK (CONTINUING)
> Roll call, everyone.
> (beat)
> Alvarez?

A girl raises her hand.

> MR. BLANK (CONTINUING)
> Anderson?

A boy raises his hand.

Jason stares straight ahead, tuning everyone out. He opens his notebook and begins to doodle.

                    MR. BLANK (CONTINUING)
Clark?

No one answers or raises a hand.

                    MR. BLANK (CONTINUING)
Clark? Adam Clark?

Jason stops doodling and looks around.

                    MR. BLANK (CONTINUING)
Adam Clark?

Adam runs into the classroom.

                    MR. BLANK (CONTINUING)
Homeroom is eight thirty sharp, Clark.

                    ADAM
I'm sorry, Mr. Blank. It won't happen again.

                    MR. BLANK
I called your name three times. I thought I had
Tourette's. Please have a seat.

Mr. Blank continues with the roll call.

Adam looks around the classroom. He spots an empty seat in
front of Jason. Adam jets over to the empty seat and sits down.

                    JASON
    Hi, sexy.

Adam turns around.

                    ADAM
    Hey, there.

                    JASON
    I can't stop thinking of you.

Adam smiles at Jason.

                JASON (CONTINUING)
    Do you want to cut class next period?

                    ADAM
    Are you nuts? It's the first day after spring break.

                    JASON
    Who's going to find out?

                MR. BLANK (O.S.)
    Sinclair? Cassandra Sinclair?

                    KIKI (O.S.)
        (annoyed)
    For the tenth time, Mr. Blank. It's Kiki.

Jason turns to Kiki's voice.

> MR. BLANK
> (sarcastic tone)
> My apologies, Kiki. I'll start over. Sinclair? Kiki
> Sinclair?

> KIKI
> That's much better.

She raises her hand.

> KIKI (CONTINUING)
> Present.

> JASON
> On second thought, I think we better stay.

INT. MONTCLAIR HIGH SCHOOL/HALLWAY - DAY

The bell rings, and the STUDENTS exit the classroom. Adam and Jason walk out together and bump into Amanda.

> AMANDA
> Hey, guys, how's it going?

> ADAM
> Hey, sis.

> JULIAN (O.S.)
> These kids are annoying.

All three turn to Julian's voice.

                    AMANDA
Hi, Julian.

                    JULIAN
Hey there, sexy.

                    KIKI (O.S.)
Hey, yourself.

All four turn to Kiki's voice.

                    KIKI (CONTINUING)
Hi, Amanda. I am so sorry about Kevin. Are you
OK?

                    AMANDA
I'm OK, thanks. What about you? Are you OK?

                    KIKI
Uh, yeah, why?

                    JULIAN
Cassandra, weren't you his friend too?

                    KIKI
        (to Julian)
I remember you. You were at my party.

She looks over to Jason.

KIKI (CONTINUING)
I see that there is another one.

JULIAN
I remember you, too.
(beat)
Hey, is it true that you saw someone running from the scene of the crime?

KIKI
Yeah, I saw everything.

JULIAN
Everything?

The bell rings.

AMANDA
Shit, we're going to be late for class.

JASON
Can someone tell me where room four twenty-five is?

KIKI
World history?

JASON
Yeah.

KIKI
Follow me. I'm in that class.

ADAM

So am I.

JULIAN

Well, can someone tell me where room one nineteen
is, or should I wander around aimlessly?

AMANDA
(laughing)
I'll take you. I know where it is.

Kiki puts her arms around Adam and Jason.

KIKI

Follow me, boys. It's time to walk momma to class.

She turns back to Amanda and Julian.

KIKI (CONTINUING)
Amanda, lunch period? Same time, same place?

INT. MONTCLAIR HIGH SCHOOL/LUNCHROOM - DAY

The group is sitting at the same lunch table.

KIKI
(to Amanda)
How are you dealing with everything?

AMANDA

Dealing with what?

                    KIKI
What do mean, with what? How are you dealing
with Kevin's death? Everyone in school is talking
about it. They're having a memorial for him, Rick
Hyde, and Jake Hanson in the auditorium. It's freaky
shit, right?

                    AMANDA
Kiki, I don't want to talk about it, OK?

                    KIKI
OMG, I am so sorry. This must bring back
memories of your mom, right?

                    AMANDA
Are you kidding me? How can you even compare
the two?

                    KIKI
OK, relax. You know, your bitchiness is unladylike.
How are you supposed to keep a man with that
attitude?

Amanda turns away from Kiki.

                    KIKI (CONTINUING)
Amanda, what happened to us? We used to be really
good friends.

AMANDA

Friends? You weren't thinking about our friendship
when you were fucking Kevin behind my back.

Julian, Jason, and Adam hear this and stop eating.

KIKI

Are you kidding? I've never slept with Kevin.

Jason leans into Julian.

JASON
(whispering to Julian)
Drama…Love it.

KIKI

Who told you that?

AMANDA

C'mon, Kiki, I'm not stupid.

KIKI

Kevin and I were friends and nothing more. Plus, I
was dating your brother until he decided to question
his sexuality.

JULIAN

Imagine that.

                    JASON
          (to himself)
     I can see why.

                    KIKI
          (to Adam)
     It's true.

Adam remains silent.

                    AMANDA
     You're such a bitch. Not everyone knows, OK?

                    KIKI
     Honey, everyone knows.

                    AMANDA
     That's not the point.

                    KIKI
     You know, if you're so upset with me, why did you
     come to my party?

Amanda grabs her things and gets up from the table.

                    KIKI (CONTINUING)
     Where are you going?

                    AMANDA
     Guys, I'm going to head back to class.

                    JULIAN
    I'll walk with you.

Julian gets up from the table and follows Amanda.

INT. MONTCLAIR HIGH SCHOOL/HALLWAY - DAY

Amanda quickly walks out of the lunchroom.

                    JULIAN
    Hey, wait up.

Amanda stops.

                    JULIAN (CONTINUING)
    Are you OK?

                    AMANDA
    No.

                    JULIAN
    Can I ask you a question? Why did you bring me to
    her party?

                    AMANDA
    I don't know.

                    JULIAN
    Yes, you do. I think you wanted to get Kevin jealous.
    That's why you brought me.

Amanda turns away from Julian.

                    AMANDA
You're right. I'm sorry. I wanted to show him that he
didn't break me, but now I feel so guilty about it.

                    JULIAN
Why should you feel guilty? You know, sometimes
life throws a curve ball at you. In Kevin's case, it was
a hundred-and-fifty-foot drop.

                    AMANDA
What?

                    JULIAN
Never mind.

Julian sees Peter and Nathan heading their way.

            JULIAN (CONTINUING)
Here comes your dad with Sheriff Nobody.

Peter approaches Amanda and Julian.

                    PETER
        (to Amanda)
Hey, sweetheart. How are you?

                    AMANDA
I'm fine.

                    PETER

Are you sure?

                    AMANDA

Yeah, I'm OK.

                    PETER

Where's Cassandra?

                    JULIAN

She's in the lunchroom with Adam and Jason. Is
there a problem?

                    NATHAN

I just need to question her again. I may also need to
question you and Amanda again later.

Kiki exits the lunchroom. Peter stops her.

                    PETER

Cassandra, Sheriff McFadden needs to speak to you.
Please come with me to my office.

                    KIKI
              (grabbing her bag)
For what? I don't have any.

                    NATHAN

What are you talking about? Any what? I need to ask
you some more questions regarding Kevin O'Hare.

KIKI

I told you everything.

NATHAN

Based on recent evidence, I need to ask you a few more questions.

KIKI

What recent evidence?

Adam and Jason exit the lunchroom and approach Peter and Nathan.

PETER

Let's talk in my office.

JULIAN

Mr. Clark, if it helps, I can go with you and answer any questions that the sheriff may have.

NATHAN

Actually, that's not a bad idea. We can do it all in one shot.

ADAM

Dad, what's going on?

PETER

I can't discuss this right now, Adam. First off, you and Jason need to get back to class. You three, come with me to my office.

INT. MONTCLAIR HIGH SCHOOL/PETER'S OFFICE - DAY

Peter sits behind his desk while Nathan questions the trio.

> NATHAN
> Julian, after the altercation with Kevin, where did
> you go next?

> JULIAN
> Amanda took me home.

> AMANDA
> Yes, that's true.

> NATHAN
> And neither one of you saw anyone else?

> AMANDA & JULIAN
> No.

> KIKI
> Sheriff, what's this all about?

> NATHAN
> Cassandra, what made you go after Kevin?

She is reluctant to answer the question.

> NATHAN (CONTINUING)
> Cassandra?

                    KIKI
Yes?

                    NATHAN
Can you answer the question? Why did you go after
Kevin?

                    KIKI
I wanted to see if he was going after Amanda.

                    NATHAN
Were you and Kevin seeing each other?

She does not respond.

                    AMANDA
Well?

                    PETER
Amanda, let the sheriff do the questioning.

                    KIKI
Yes.

Amanda leans into Kiki.

                    AMANDA
You're a cunt.

                    JULIAN
Whoa…
        (to Kiki)
How do you bounce back from that?

                    PETER
Amanda!

                    KIKI
It just happened, Amanda. We didn't do it to hurt
you.

                    NATHAN
You mentioned in your initial report that you saw
someone standing by the guardrail.

                    KIKI
Yes, and whoever it was ran when they saw my
headlights.

                    NATHAN
What did the individual look like?

Julian looks over to Kiki.

                    KIKI
It was hard to tell, because the person was wearing
black. Sheriff, what's going on? I thought this was
ruled out as a drunk-driving accident.

NATHAN

Not anymore. There was an autopsy conducted on
Kevin's body, along with the two other boys. The
coroner concluded that his head injuries were not
caused by the car accident. His injuries occurred
before the accident.

PETER

What are you saying?

NATHAN

His accident *was* no accident. It was made to look
that way.

Julian continues to stare at Kiki.

PETER

Julian, are you OK?

Julian snaps out of his daze.

JULIAN

It's scary, you know?

PETER

Why do you say that?

JULIAN

Because, you never know when it can happen again.

INT. MONTCLAIR HIGH SCHOOL/REGISTRAR'S OFFICE - DAY

Peter's office door opens, and Julian walks out. He has a worried look on his face.

INT. MONTCLAIR HIGH SCHOOL/HALLWAY - DAY

Julian walks into a hallway full of STUDENTS. He takes out his iPhone and calls Jason.

> JULIAN
> Hey, where are you?...No, don't go to your class...
> Meet me at the football field in ten minutes.

He hangs up the phone.

INT. MONTCLAIR HIGH SCHOOL/PETER'S OFFICE - DAY

Peter sits behind his desk searching the Internet.

He types John Montanoro's name into the search engine.

A number of results appear on the screen. He clicks on a few links before coming across a news article for a company called Montanoro Real Estate.

Peter scrolls down the article.

                           PETER
              (to himself)
          Real estate developer John Montanoro, CEO
          of Montanoro Real Estate, files for bankruptcy
          following the collapse of his company...

The article reveals a picture of John in a business suit sitting
behind a desk.

Peter scrolls down the article again and clicks on another link.

This time he sees the photos of a party. Peter scrolls farther
down and sees a picture of John and Nancy. They are smiling
and embracing each other.

He then sees another picture of John standing in the middle of
the party with three teenage boys. The boys are triplets.

                           PETER
              (to himself)
            There's another one?

Peter takes out Julian and Jason's certificates of immunization
and looks through them. He types the name DR. ROBERT
CORRAL into the search engine.

EXT. MONTCLAIR HIGH SCHOOL/FOOTBALL FIELD -
DAY

Julian and Jason are under the bleachers.

                    JASON
I can't do that.

He pauses.

                    JASON (CONTINUING)
You said that it would be different this time.

                    JULIAN
We both knew that it would come to this. We don't
have a choice now. This is our opportunity.

                    JASON
Yes, we do. We have a choice.

                    JULIAN
We need to move on with our plan. There's no
turning back now.

                    JASON
We'll only end up in a foster home, and that's a fate
worse than death.

                    JULIAN
For once, think. We turn eighteen in a few months,
and we have other relatives that live in New York.

                    JASON
They have no idea where we are.

                    JULIAN
Not yet.

Jason remains silent.

                    JULIAN (CONTINUING)
OK, maybe this time we were sloppy.

                    JASON
We? No, you were sloppy. Your impatience got the
best of you, just like it always does.

                    JULIAN
What are you suggesting we do? Do you not want to
go through with it?

                    JASON
I finally found happiness, and you can't deal with it.

                    JULIAN
Are you shitting me? Do you really think that Adam
cares for you?

                    JASON
Yeah, I do.

                    JULIAN
You're delusional. Adam doesn't care about you.

Jason looks angrily at Julian.

JULIAN (CONTINUING)
Oh, I'm sorry. Did I hit a nerve? He's only playing
you until he moves on to the next guy.

JASON
That's not true.

JULIAN
Yeah, keep repeating that to yourself.

Julian leans in closer to Jason.

JULIAN (CONTINUING)
You're not getting in the way of this. Don't try.

JASON
I can't do this to him. He doesn`t deserve it.

JULIAN
I'm not going to discuss this with you anymore.
Only two will be left standing. The rest are
expendable. End of discussion, James.

JASON
What did you just call me?

Julian doesn't respond.

JASON (CONTINUING)
I'm not him, and I never will be. Get that through
your twisted little head.

                    JULIAN
I didn't mean it that way.

                    JASON
I've always had to compete with him my entire life.
It was always you two. You guys never cared about
me.

                    JULIAN
You're my brother, and I would never let anyone get
in between us. Point blank, Adam has to go, Jason.

Jason starts to run. Julian chases after him and tackles him.

                    JULIAN (CONTINUING)
Do you trust me?

Jason does not answer.

                    JULIAN (CONTINUING)
I said, do you trust me?

                    JASON
I trust you.

                    JULIAN
Then understand this: romance only lasts until
reality sets in.

Jason starts crying.

JASON

She invited me over to her place tonight.

Julian wipes the tears from Jason's face.

JULIAN

She, as in Kiki?

JASON

Yeah.

JULIAN

Perfect. Just the both of you?

JASON

Adam will be there too. Our teacher wants us to
work on a project together.

JULIAN

Then, it happens tonight…

Julian stops in midsentence. He smiles and looks at Jason.

JASON

What's wrong?

JULIAN

I've got an idea.

                         JASON
    What?

Julian helps Jason up and embraces him.

                         JULIAN
         I want you to know that it will always be you and
         me.

Julian kisses his brother on the cheek and walks in the opposite
direction.

                         JASON
              (yelling)
         Where are you going?

INT. MONTCLAIR HIGH SCHOOL/LIBRARY - DAY

Julian feverishly types into the computer.

The look on his face tells us that he is very pleased with his
results.

Julian hits the print button on the web browser. He takes the
pages from the printer and goes through them.

We see that he has printed a news article, a page from a yearbook,
and a telephone listing.

He walks down an empty aisle and takes out his iPhone.

He presses star sixty-seven and proceeds to dial a phone number.

> JULIAN
> Hello. May I please speak to the parents of Justin McBride?

Julian pauses.

> JULIAN
> Hello, Mrs. McBride. I'm calling from the *Montclair Journal*, and we are doing another story on your son Justin…

Julian pauses.

> JULIAN (CONTINUING)
> I know, ma'am. I do apologize, and I know how sensitive this is, but we wanted to tell your son's side of the story.

Julian looks around. The aisle is still empty.

He continues.

> JULIAN (CONTINUING)
> You stated in your last interview that your son was not drinking the night that he got into the car accident that claimed a woman's life.

Julian pauses.

JULIAN (CONTINUING)
Oh, I'm sorry…

He pulls out the printed article, written by BEN STURMAN.

JULIAN (CONTINUING)
My name is Ben Sturman. I'm the reporter who
interviewed you a week after your son's car accident
claimed the life of Samantha Clark.

INT. MONTCLAIR HIGH SCHOOL/PETER'S OFFICE - DAY

Peter picks up the phone and calls Nathan.

PETER
Nathan McFadden, please…Nate, Peter here. Can
you come by my office again? Say around three
thirty?…Great, thanks. See you then.

He hangs up the phone. There is a knock on the door.

PETER (CONTINUING)
Come in.

Carmen enters.

CARMEN
You're going to be late for the memorial.

PETER
What?

                    CARMEN

The memorial. We're gathering in the auditorium at
one thirty, remember?

Peter has a blank look on his face.

                    CARMEN (CONTINUING)
          Mr. Clark?

                    PETER
          That's right.
              (beat)
          What time is it now?

                    CARMEN
          One fifteen.

INT. MONTCLAIR HIGH SCHOOL/HALLWAY - DAY

The bell rings, and the STUDENTS exit the classrooms. Adam
goes to his locker and puts his books inside. He turns and bumps
right into the twins.

                    ADAM
          Hey guys, what's up?

                    JULIAN
          What's going on? Why is everyone heading to the
          auditorium?

ADAM

They're having a memorial for Kevin O'Hare, Rick
Hyde, and Jake Hanson.

Julian and Jason do not respond.

ADAM (CONTINUING)

You know? The three varsity football players who
were killed over the weekend?

JULIAN

Why?

ADAM

Why, what?

JULIAN

Why would they be having a memorial for them?
Weren't they alcoholics?

ADAM

That's not the point, Julian. I grew up with these
guys, and regardless what they were, what happened
to them was pretty fucked up.

JULIAN

Be that as it may, they were still drinking and
driving.

Adam looks at Julian in disbelief.

ADAM

I have to go. I'm going to be late.

JULIAN

Is attendance mandatory?

ADAM
(sarcastically)

Uh, yeah.

JULIAN

Can we walk with you?

ADAM

You know what? I think I'm going to finish up here
first.

JULIAN

Are you sure? We can wait.

ADAM

It's OK. Go ahead. I'll meet up with the both of you
inside.

Julian proceeds to walk away. Jason stays behind.

JASON

I'm sorry about that.

ADAM

Your brother's a bit cold.

                    JASON
He can be at times.

Jason leans in and kisses Adam on the lips. Adam pushes him
away.

                    JASON (CONTINUING)
What's wrong?

                    ADAM
Not here, Jason.

                    JASON
So, what?

Jason advances again. Adam stops him.

                    ADAM
Not here. Everyone is watching.

                    JASON
And?

                    ADAM
I guess you're more comfortable with it than I am.

TWO FEMALE STUDENTS walking by Adam and Jason look at
them and roll their eyes.

                    ADAM (CONTINUING)
C'mon, let's go. We're going to be late.

                    JASON
Go ahead; I'll catch up with you. Save me a seat.

Adam passes the two female students as he enters the auditorium.

              JASON (O.S.) (CONTINUING)
Isn't this school supposed to be a grenade-free
environment?

Both girls turn around. Jason slicks one of the girls in the ear.

                 FEMALE STUDENT 1
You asshole!

                    ADAM
        (walking away)
Next time take a picture, bitch!

Jason enters the auditorium.

INT. MONTCLAIR HIGH SCHOOL/AUDITORIUM - DAY

The entire STUDENT BODY is seated.

Peter walks onto the auditorium stage.

Peter taps the microphone, and a screeching sound penetrates
the auditorium. The students cover their ears.

> PETER
> OK, everyone settle down. I'm sure that your
> eardrums are still intact.

He pauses.

> PETER (CONTINUING)
> As many of you already know, an unfortunate event
> occurred over the weekend.

Peter looks around the auditorium.

> PETER (CONTINUING)
> This weekend, Kevin O'Hare, Rick Hyde, and Jake
> Hanson…

Peter is now looking directly at Julian.

> PETER (CONTINUING)
> Fell victim to an accident that claimed their lives.

Peter sees a smirk on Julian's face.

> PETER (CONTINUING)
> They were not only part of our community, they
> were part of our student body. They were our
> friends, our classmates, but most of all, they were
> part of our family, and they will be deeply missed.

Peter pauses.

> PETER (CONTINUING)
> If anyone has anything to say, please feel free to
> come up on stage.

Peter looks around the auditorium. Everyone is silent.

> PETER (CONTINUING)
> I am now going to hand the microphone over to
> Cassandra Sinclair.

Kiki walks onto the stage and takes the microphone from Peter.

> KIKI
> Thank you, Mr. Clark.
> (beat)
> It's Kiki, by the way.

Peter stands behind Kiki as he continues to look at Julian.

> KIKI (CONTINUING)
> Hi. I'm sure many of you know me—

> MALE VOICE (O.S.)
> Crack whore!

> KIKI
> (whining)
> Mr. Clark, they called me a crack whore. Do
> something.

Everyone in the auditorium starts to laugh. Peter takes the microphone away from Kiki.

>
PETER
Hey, let's act like adults, not children. Show some respect to your fellow classmate. Keep it up, and you'll all be staying here after hours instead of being dismissed early. It's up to you.

Everyone quiets down.

PETER (CONTINUING)
Thank you.

Peter hands the microphone back to Kiki.

KIKI
As I was saying, many of you know me, and many of you know that Kevin and I were friends…

We now see Amanda from Kiki's POV.

KIKI (CONTINUING)
Really good friends…

Kiki rolls her eyes at Amanda and continues.

KIKI (CONTINUING)
His death, along with Rick Hyde and Jake Hanson, was a shock to all of us in the community…

From Peter's POV, we see Julian get up from his seat and casually walk out of the auditorium.

Peter jumps off the stage. All heads turn to Peter as he runs out of the auditorium.

INT. MONTCLAIR HIGH SCHOOL/HALLWAY - DAY

Julian turns to the sound of a bursting door. He sees Peter standing in the middle of the hallway.

> PETER
> Where do you think you're going?

Julian turns and continues to walk away.

> JULIAN
> I'm not going to mourn over someone I didn't know.

> PETER
> I don't know how they did things at Lakeview
> High…

Julian stops walking.

> PETER (CONTINUING)
> But in Montclair High, we do things differently.

Julian turns and walks toward Peter.

                    JULIAN
        (sarcastically)
What are you doing? Checking up on us?

Julian and Peter are now face to face.

                    JULIAN (CONTINUING)
Who did you speak to? Principal Huot?

                    PETER
No, I spoke to his successor. Unfortunately, your
former principal died in a car accident.

                    JULIAN
Well, he did like to drink and drive.

                    PETER
I don't think that's funny.

                    JULIAN
Why? Too close for comfort?

                    PETER
You little prick!

                    JULIAN
I will admit, even I couldn't figure out how you did
it.

                    PETER
Did what?

JULIAN

Come on, Peter. Now you're playing with my
intelligence.

Peter pushes Julian against the wall.

PETER

Look, you little shit, I don't know what you're getting
at—

JULIAN

Yes, you do.

PETER

I don't know what it is that you think you know
about me, but—

JULIAN

Tell me about Justin McBride.

Peter is taken aback.

PETER

Justin McBride?

JULIAN

Yeah, you know, the kid who was killed along with
your wife on New Year's Eve.

PETER

How did you find out about that?

JULIAN
According to his mother—

PETER
You spoke to his mother?

JULIAN
Hey, you called my old high school. I'd say that makes us even.

Peter grabs Julian by the shirt and pulls Julian closer to him.

PETER
I don't know what she told you, but what happened was an accident.

JULIAN
Oh, yeah, an accident. A kid from the wrong side of town, and it's automatically assumed that he was the one who caused the accident.

Peter does not respond.

JULIAN (CONTINUING)
Wasn't he seeing Amanda? That's what his mother told me. And you didn't like him, did you?

Peter lets go of his grip.

JULIAN (CONTINUING)
It's unfortunate that you killed a student with a four
point oh GPA without a history of drinking, and
you're the one who gets off scot-free. Who did you
have to suck to pull that one off?

Peter grabs Julian by both of his arms and slams him against the
lockers.

JULIAN (CONTINUING)
You're hurting me.

PETER
I don't know what kind of game you're playing, but
it's not going to end well for you.

JULIAN
Are you threatening me?

PETER
You may have my kids and everyone else fooled, but
not me.

JULIAN
Fooled by what? What are you accusing me of?

PETER
Where were you last night?

JULIAN
With your daughter. Go and ask her.

PETER

Where was your brother?

JULIAN

Probably banging your son. Go and ask him.

Peter grips Julian's shirt once again.

PETER

(screaming)

I want you to stay away from my kids. If you don't,
you'll regret it!

JULIAN

What was that? I can't hear you.

PETER

(screaming louder)

Stay away from my kids, or you'll regret it!

AMANDA (O.S.)

Dad, what are you doing?

Peter stops screaming and turns to Amanda.

He sees that the entire STUDENT BODY and the FACULTY are
standing in the hallway looking at him.

Peter releases his grip on Julian.

PETER
(to everyone)
I'm sorry. I know this looks worse than what it is.

JULIAN
(to Peter)
Don't touch me. You threatened me, and everyone heard you.

PETER
Julian, let's call your father, and we'll straighten this out.

Peter grabs Julian's arm. Julian pulls away.

JULIAN
I said, don't touch me. I'm not going anywhere with you unless it's being supervised by a faculty member.

PETER
I'll have Carmen stay with you until your father arrives.

JULIAN
You do that.

INT. MONTCLAIR HIGH SCHOOL/REGISTRAR'S OFFICE - DAY

Julian sits with his arms crossed. He stares straight ahead while Carmen sits at her desk eating.

She looks over to him, and Julian gives her a dirty look.

                    JULIAN
          Did you speak to my father?

                    CARMEN
          Yes, he'll be here any minute.

                    JULIAN
          Really? How long ago did you speak to him?

                    CARMEN
          Around five minutes ago.

                    JULIAN
          Five minutes ago, you were on the phone laughing
          and speaking Spanish to one of your Puerto Rican
          friends. I doubt you were speaking to him.

Carmen stares blankly at Julian as John enters the office.

                    JOHN
          Julian, what happened?

                    JULIAN
          Take me home.

Julian gets up from the seat and gathers his things. Peter comes
out of his office.

PETER

Hello, Mr. Montanoro. Can I have a word with you?

JOHN

Julian, wait for me in the car.

Julian leaves the office.

PETER

I just want to clear a few things up. I know I lost my
temper with Julian—

JOHN

You don't have to defend yourself. I already know
what happened.

John leaves the office.

INT. MONTCLAIR HIGH SCHOOL/PETER'S OFFICE - DAY

Peter sits silently at his desk. There is a knock on the door.

PETER

Come in.

Amanda and Adam enter his office.

PETER (CONTINUING)

Hey guys, what's up? What are you still doing here?
Why didn't you leave during early dismissal?

AMANDA

I had swimming practice.

ADAM

I was just hanging around.

PETER

With Jason?

ADAM

No, Dad. I was waiting for Amanda. I'm giving her a ride home.

AMANDA

Dad, what happened between you and Julian today?

PETER

It was nothing.

AMANDA

You were shouting like a madman, Dad.

PETER

Amanda, let it go.

AMANDA

How can I? The whole school saw you acting like a crazy person.

PETER

I was not acting crazy.

ADAM

That's not what it looked like. Everyone's talking
about it, Dad.

Peter gets up from his chair and goes over to them.

PETER

I'm only looking out for the both of you. I don't trust
those kids.

AMANDA

That's the way it's always been, Dad. You never like,
or trust, anyone.

PETER

That's not true.

ADAM

You didn't like me dating Kiki.

PETER

That's because I hear that she's always high, and
drunk. The only reason why I haven't expelled her
is because I've yet to physically catch her in the act.
And you're gay—

ADAM

That's not the point.

AMANDA

What about Kevin and Justin? You didn't like either
of them.

PETER

C'mon, why did you have to bring up Justin?
Julian—

AMANDA

Julian's not the enemy here. You are.

PETER

What?

AMANDA

You are your own worst enemy. Your drinking is
getting the best of you, and it's getting out of hand.

PETER

Amanda, this is not about my drinking.

AMANDA

The sad part is that everyone knows about it, and
there's nothing I can do.
(to Adam)
I'll wait for you in the car.

                    PETER
That's not fair, Amanda.

Amanda leaves Peter's office.

                    PETER (CONTINUING)
Amanda.

                    ADAM
Dad, not like this. You've done enough screaming
for the day.

                    PETER
What? Are you judging me too?

                    ADAM
No, that's what psychiatrists are for.

                    PETER
Nice one, Adam.

There is a knock on the door, and Nathan enters.

                    PETER (CONTINUING)
     (to Nathan)
Nate, great timing.
     (to Adam)
I'll see you later?

                    ADAM
     Sure.

Adam leaves the office.

                    PETER
     I'm glad you're here. I've got a few things to tell you.

                    NATHAN
     I've got a few things to tell *you*.

INT. MONTANORO HOME/JULIAN'S BEDROOM - DAY

Jason is sitting on Julian's bed. They are both dressed the same.

                    JULIAN
     Are you ready?

                    JASON
     Why can't I do this?

                    JULIAN
     Because you'll only fuck it up. I'm doing this, so
     drop it.

                    JASON
     I won't fuck it up.

                    JULIAN
     Yes, you will. Did they come home?

JASON

Yeah, I saw their car pull up ten minutes ago.

JULIAN

Was he with them?

JASON

No.

JULIAN

Remember to act calm and cool. Don't flame and butch it up.

Jason shoves Julian.

JULIAN (CONTINUING)

What the fuck?

JASON

I'm tired of your stupid comments.

JULIAN

You've got gumption. I'm impressed.

Julian approaches Jason and sizes him up. Jason clenches his fists.

JULIAN (CONTINUING)

Let's go.

They grab their backpacks and leave the room.

INT. MONTCLAIR HIGH SCHOOL/PETER'S OFFICE - DAY

Peter slams his hand on his desk.

> PETER
> You've got to be kidding me. He's lying. That didn't happen at all!

> NATHAN
> He's not saying that you hit him in any way, only that you roughed him up.

> PETER
> Nate, I did not rough him up.

> NATHAN
> Peter, I want to believe you. Really, I do, but you've had altercations with your students before.

> PETER
> Nathan, these kids are hiding something, and so are their parents. I just know it.

> NATHAN
> Peter, what are you talking about?

> PETER
> I checked them out.

> NATHAN
> And?

PETER
I called their former physician, Dr. Robert Corral.
He signed their certificate of immunization—

NATHAN
How did you get his number?

PETER
I Googled it.

NATHAN
You Googled it? I'm afraid to ask…What did he say?

PETER
I spoke to the new physician in charge. Their
primary care physician has been missing for over a
year…

NATHAN
(touches his forehead)
I have a headache—

PETER
He told me that they attended Lakeview High. I
called Lakeview High…

Nathan takes a deep breath and sits down.

PETER (CONTINUING)
I was told that the former principal died in a car accident. He also said that the parents took them out of school unexpectedly and moved away. No one has seen them since.

NATHAN
Get to the point.

PETER
I think the parents are hiding something. I also think these kids had something to do with the disappearances as well.

NATHAN
Are you listening to yourself?

PETER
Did you know that they had another son? They're triplets, Nate, triplets.

NATHAN
How did you find this out?

JOHN
I saw their picture in a news article that was written about their father.

NATHAN
OK, you need to stop. You're invading this family's privacy.

                    PETER

Nate, these kids are dangerous. I think they killed
Kevin and his friends. They've probably done this
before.

                    NATHAN

You know what I see? I see a man whose obsessing.
We've gone down this road before.

                    PETER

It's different this time.

                    NATHAN

No, it's not. You did the same thing with your former
student, Justin McBride, and look what happened to
him.

                    PETER

That was an accident.

                    NATHAN

I know it was, but you need to relax, because I won't
be able to get you out of another jam like I did last
time.

Peter looks the other way and does not respond.

              NATHAN (CONTINUING)

OK, I've got to get back to the station. Cool off, you
got it?

                    PETER
    Yeah, I got it.

Nathan gets up and leaves. Peter opens his desk drawer and takes
out a small flask.

He opens it and puts it to his lips. He stops, puts the cover back
on, and puts it back in the drawer.

                    PETER (CONTINUING)
    Fuck.

INT. MONTANORO HOME/FOYER - DAY

Julian and Jason slowly creep down the stairs. Julian peeks into
the living room and sees that John is watching TV.

They sneak out the front door without John noticing them.

EXT. MONTANORO HOME/STREET - DAY

                    JULIAN
    Did he see us?

                    JASON
    No.

They reach Amanda's front porch.

EXT. CLARK HOME/PORCH - DAY

Jason walks up to the front door.

> JULIAN
> OK, you know what you have to do, right?

> JASON
> Yes, already! Just hurry up.

Jason knocks on the door as Julian runs to the backyard.

Amanda opens the door.

> AMANDA
> Hey, Julian. How are you?

> JASON
> I'm doing good. How are you?

> AMANDA
> I'm sorry about my dad.

> JASON
> It's all good, I guess.

EXT. CLARK HOME/BACKYARD - DAY

Julian looks around. He opens his backpack, pulls out a pair of gloves, and puts them on.

He walks cautiously toward the kitchen door and turns the knob. He slowly opens the door.

EXT. CLARK HOME/PORCH - DAY

Jason sees the kitchen door opening behind Amanda. Julian sneaks inside and slowly closes the door.

> AMANDA
> Do you want to come inside? My dad won't be home until later.

She turns to go back inside, but Jason quickly turns her around. We see Julian from Jason's POV walking slowly toward the stairs.

> JASON
> I don't think that's a good idea. After everything that's happened today, I just wanted to apologize.

> AMANDA
> For what? It wasn't your fault.

Jason looks back at Julian. Julian gives him the thumbs-up and slowly proceeds up the stairs.

Amanda steps out onto the porch, leaving the door slightly ajar.

> AMANDA (CONTINUING)
> I'm really glad that you came by.

                         JASON
Um, really?

Amanda leans closer to kiss him. Jason backs away.

                         AMANDA
What's wrong?

INT. CLARK HOME/STAIRWAY - DAY

Julian reaches the top of the stairs, and takes a peek down the hallway. The lights are off.

INT. CLARK HOME/HALLWAY - DAY

Julian creeps down the hallway and checks out the first bedroom. He looks inside and sees that it's Amanda's room.

He checks the next bedroom. The lights are on, but no one is inside. He sees that it's Adam's room.

He reaches the end of the hall. There are two rooms left, and both of the doors are closed.

He slowly turns the knob to one of the doors, and it is locked. He then hears the sound of the toilet flushing from behind the door.

Julian backs up and turns the knob to the other door. He quickly goes into the bedroom as Adam comes out of the bathroom.

EXT. CLARK HOME/PORCH - DAY

Jason turns his back to Amanda.

                    AMANDA
        What's wrong?

He closes his eyes and takes a deep breath. He opens his eyes and faces her.

                    JASON
        Nothing's wrong.

He pulls her closer and kisses her.

INT. CLARK HOME/PETER'S BEDROOM - DAY

Julian looks around Peter's bedroom.

He places the backpack on Peter's bed, opens the closet door, and looks inside. He fumbles through the suits, jackets, and pants.

He takes a blue sweater, a trench coat, and a belt from the closet and shoves them into the backpack. He keeps fumbling through the closet and comes across a flask. He shakes it and hears that it's full.

He goes through the closet one more time. He finds a straight-razor kit. He takes the razor and puts it in the backpack. He closes the closet door.

He goes to the bedroom door and slowly opens it. He peeks through and leaves the room.

INT. CLARK HOME/HALLWAY - DAY

Julian walks slowly down the hallway just as Adam walks out of his bedroom.

                    ADAM
Hey—

                    JULIAN
Jason. It's me, Jason.

                    ADAM
Dude, I knew it was you. What are you doing up here?

                    JULIAN
I was looking for you. I didn't see you up here, so I was going to head out to Kiki's.

                    ADAM
Do you know how to get there?

                    JULIAN
No, I don't. I was going to ask your sister to give me directions.

                    ADAM
Hold on, let me turn on the light.

Julian puts his hands behind his back and quickly removes the gloves. He puts one in each back pocket.

                    ADAM (CONTINUING)
          That's better.

Adam leans in to kiss him. Julian pushes him away.

                    JULIAN
          What do you think you're doing?

                    ADAM
          I want to kiss you.

Adam leans in again. Julian backs away.

                    JULIAN
          I don't feel comfortable knowing that your sister is
          downstairs.

                    ADAM
          Like she really gives a shit.

Adam leans in and starts kissing him. Julian tries his best to push him away, but Adam comes on strong.

Julian shoves him. Adam hits the nightstand and knocks over a vase.

EXT. CLARK HOME/PORCH - DAY

Amanda hears the vase shattering.

INT. CLARK HOME/HALLWAY - DAY

                    AMANDA (O.S.)
          Adam, are you OK?

                    ADAM
               (to Amanda)
          Yeah, I'm OK.

He goes over to Julian.

                    ADAM (CONTINUING)
          Dude, what's your problem?

                    AMANDA (O.S.)
          What happened?

                    JULIAN
          Don't tell her I'm here. You'll only embarrass me.

                    ADAM
          Jason, who cares if she knows you're here?

                    JULIAN
          I care.

Julian pushes Adam against the wall and kisses him.

Julian stops.

JULIAN (CONTINUING)
I'll meet you outside, OK?

ADAM
Damn, you're a great kisser.

JULIAN
That's good to know.

ADAM
Are you OK? You look pale.

JULIAN
I'm OK, I'm OK. I'll wait for you outside.

Julian quickly exits the hallway and goes down the stairs.

EXT. CLARK HOME/PORCH - DAY

AMANDA
I'm going to check up on Adam.

Amanda goes inside. Jason watches her as she goes up the stairs. Julian pops out from behind the front door.

JASON
You were there this whole time?

JULIAN
Take this.

He opens his backpack and takes out the blue sweater.

> JULIAN (CONTINUING)
> Shove this into your backpack and wait for your boy
> toy by the driveway. Go, now!

Jason leaves as Amanda and Adam exit the house. Adam looks at Julian.

> ADAM
> Hey…

> JULIAN
> What up, yo?

> ADAM
> Where's your brother?

> JULIAN
> He's waiting for you by your car.

> ADAM
> I'm out of here, Amanda. Jason and I are headed off
> to Kiki's.

> AMANDA
> Don't come home too late.

> ADAM
> I won't.

Julian embraces Amanda.

> JULIAN
> Now, where were we?

INT. MONTANORO HOME/LIVING ROOM - NIGHT

The TV is playing loudly as John lies asleep on the sofa. He suddenly awakens and looks around the living room. He turns the TV off.

INT. MONTANORO HOME/FOYER - NIGHT

John turns on the light.

> JOHN
> Julian?

There is no answer.

> JOHN (CONTINUING)
> Jason?

There is no answer.

The phone rings, and he picks it up.

> JOHN (CONTINUING)
> Hello?

> NANCY (O.S.)
> Hey, it's me.

JOHN
Are you OK? How are you feeling?

NANCY (O.S.)
I was thinking…I was thinking about the day we
found out I was pregnant…You were so happy. Do
you remember?

JOHN
That was one of the happiest days of my life.

NANCY (O.S.)
Then the doctor told me that I was having triplets.
I remember the look on your face when the doctor
told us they were boys. It made me happy to see you
happy.

JOHN
What's wrong, Nance?

NANCY (O.S.)
I don't know what I gave birth to, John. They're like
a cancer that keeps on spreading. I can't live like this
anymore.

JOHN
I don't love them, Nancy. They're detestable—

NANCY (O.S.)
Do what you have to do, John. I won't stop you. I
love you.

                         JOHN
    I love you too.

He hangs up the phone.

INT. MONTANORO HOME/BASEMENT - NIGHT

John turns on the light and goes down the stairs.

He goes over to a stack of boxes and starts removing them one by
one. He reaches the bottom box and opens it.

He removes a duffel bag from inside of the box. He then takes
out the burned pieces of the baseball bats and puts them in the
bag.

He closes the bag and walks back up the stairs. He turns off the
light.

INT. KIKI'S HOME/LIVING ROOM - NIGHT

Kiki opens a bottle of wine and pours it into three wine glasses.

                         KIKI
    Drink up, ladies.

She hands the wine glasses to Jason and Adam.

Jason takes the glass and chugs down the wine. He puts the wine
glass on the table and gestures for her to pour some more.

ADAM
(to Jason)
You need to take it easy with that.

KIKI
(to Adam)
Honey, you need to remove that stick from out of
your ass and learn to have some fun.

She pours more wine into Jason's glass.

KIKI (CONTINUING)
(to Jason)
Isn't this sublime?

Adam opens his backpack and takes out his books. He places
them on the coffee table.

ADAM
OK, let's get started with this.

KIKI
Get started with what?

ADAM
Our class project. We have to—

KIKI
Oh, no, honey. Put those books away. We'll get to
that later.

                           ADAM
No, Kiki. That's not what we're here for. If we're not
going to do this, then I'm leaving.

                           JASON
            (to Adam)
No, no, we'll get to it. Let's relax a bit.

                           KIKI
Nobody puts baby in a corner.

                           ADAM
What the hell are you talking about?

Adam goes over to Jason.

                  ADAM (CONTINUING)
            (whispering to Jason)
She's fucking wasted.

                           JASON
I know. Let's stick around for a while until she sobers
up, and then we'll go.

                           KIKI
Hey, why don't you guys take your things and meet
me in my bedroom? I'll be right up. You remember
where it is? Right, Adam?

Adam rolls his eyes as he and Jason gather their things. They
leave Kiki in the living room mixing drinks.

                            152

INT. KIKI'S HOME/BEDROOM - NIGHT

Jason looks around the wildly decorated room.

                    JASON
     Nice room.

                    ADAM
     It smells like pot in here.

Kiki walks in holding a tray with drinks. She watches as Jason
takes a picture of Adam with his iPhone.

                    KIKI
     Here we go, ladies. I fixed us some cosmos.

                    JASON
     How many calories does this drink have?

                    KIKI
     Who cares?

                    JASON
     Believe me, I care. Check this out...

Jason removes his shirt. Kiki hands him a drink.

                    KIKI
          (to Jason)
     Meow, meow, kitty, kitty. Mmmm, nice.

She slowly moves her hand down along his chest and abs.

>   KIKI (CONTINUING)
>   You're hot.

She hands the other drink to Adam.

>   KIKI (CONTINUING)
>   (to Adam)
>   He's hot.

>   ADAM
>   I heard you the first time.

She hisses at Adam.

>   ADAM
>   You're a hot mess.

Jason looks up to the ceiling and sees the wooden beams that go across Kiki's bedroom.

He looks at Kiki, smiles, and gestures a "cheers" sign with his cocktail.

>   ADAM (CONTINUING)
>   (to Kiki)
>   This drink is sweet. Did you spike it?

Kiki puts her drink down and goes over to Adam. She takes his drink and places it on her nightstand. She starts to kiss him.

JASON
(to Kiki, irritated)
What are you doing?

Jason goes over to them. She stops kissing Adam and begins to kiss Jason. Jason kisses her as he looks over to Adam. Adam backs away, but Jason stops him and pulls him closer.

Kiki pushes Jason out of the way as she begins to kiss Adam again. She pulls down his zipper and puts her hand inside his pants.

We can see from the look on Jason's face that he is pissed. He goes over to them and pushes Adam out of the way. He grabs Kiki by the neck.

ADAM
(to Jason)
Are you fucking crazy!

Adam tries to pull Jason off of her, but Jason knocks him down with his free hand. Kiki tries to scratch Jason, but he blocks her.

Adam jumps Jason from behind and pulls him off of her. She falls to the floor, gasping for air.

Jason pushes Adam toward the wall. Adam quickly turns himself around, knocks Jason to the floor, and pins him down.

                    ADAM (CONTINUING)
What the fuck is wrong with you?

                         JASON
Get off of me!

                         ADAM
Not until you calm down.
    (to Kiki)
Are you OK?

                         KIKI
Yeah.
    (to Jason)
You crazy, bitch! What the fuck?

                         JASON
    (calmly)
I'm fine. Get off of me.

Adam slowly gets off of Jason. He helps him up.

                         ADAM
I think that you should go.

                         KIKI
Yeah, bitch, get the fuck out of here before I call the
cops! You're a bitch!

Jason looks over to Kiki as he puts his shirt back on. He grabs his
backpack and leaves the bedroom.

                    ADAM
          (to Kiki)
     Are you sure you're OK?

They both jump as they hear the front door slam.

INT. HOSPITAL/NANCY'S ROOM - NIGHT

Nancy is asleep. Julian enters her room wearing Peter's trench coat. He closes the door.

INT. **FLASHBACK/DREAM**/FORMER MONTANORO HOME/ KITCHEN

Nancy has finished making dinner and places the food on the table.

                    NANCY
     Jason, tell your brothers that dinner is ready.

He does not answer.

                    NANCY (CONTINUING)
          Jason?

She turns to him and sees that he is shaking a sports shake.

                    NANCY (CONTINUING)
     I don't know how you guys drink that.

JASON
The same way that we eat your food.

Nancy ignores him and calls out for Julian and James.

JULIAN
What's up?

NANCY
Your dinner is ready. Where's your dad?

John enters the kitchen and sits at the table.

JAMES
Hey, Jay, hit me up with one of those.

JASON
You can have mine.

Jason hands the shake to James. He takes a quick gulp.

NANCY
Is that all you're going to eat?

JAMES
I gotta keep in shape, but if it makes you feel any
better, I'll take a bite of Julian's chicken.

He takes a huge piece of Julian's chicken breast and stuffs it into
his mouth.

                    JOHN
Take it easy, James.

James starts coughing rapidly. He spits out his food and hits his chest.

Julian stops eating.

                    JULIAN
Are you OK?

                    NANCY
James, honey, what's wrong?

James does not respond. He grabs his throat and starts gasping for air.

                    JASON
He's choking!

John grabs him and begins to perform the Heimlich maneuver.

John continues, but his attempts are useless.

                    JASON (CONTINUING)
Get him some water!

                    JOHN
I don't think he's choking on food. He's having an allergic reaction to something. He's breaking out in hives.

Nancy, panicked, takes a steak knife from the kitchen counter.

                    JOHN (CONTINUING)
        What the hell are you doing?

                    NANCY
        Lay him on the table!

                    JOHN
        What are you going to do?

                    NANCY
        He has to breathe.

                    JULIAN
        Mom, are you crazy! Do you know what you're
        doing? Just call nine one one!

                    NANCY
        Put him on the table. We're wasting time. He needs
        to breathe.

Panicked, John places James on the table. Nancy begins to cut
into James's esophagus. Julian grabs her hand.

                    NANCY (CONTINUING)
        Get off of me. He'll die if he doesn't get air.
            (beat)
        Someone get me something…a straw, a pen casing,
        something to help him breathe. Hurry!

He lets go of Nancy, and she proceeds to cut into James. Julian fumbles through the counter drawer and hands her a pen. She loosens it and inserts the casing into the incision.

> JASON
> What's that supposed to do?

> NANCY
> It will help him breathe.

> JOHN
> Nancy, he's not breathing.

She begins blowing air into the tube.

> JOHN (CONTINUING)
> He's not breathing. He doesn't have a pulse.

Julian pushes Nancy out of the way.

> JULIAN
> He's dead.

INT. **PRESENT**/HOSPITAL/NANCY'S ROOM - NIGHT

Nancy awakens. She sees that Julian is sitting on the bed. She reaches for the buzzer, and he yanks it away from her.

He covers her mouth.

                    JULIAN
Surprised?

She slowly removes his hand and looks at him for a moment.

                    NANCY
How could I have given birth to something so vile
and tragic?

                    JULIAN
Any more adjectives?

                    NANCY
Evil.

He does not respond.

                    NANCY (CONTINUING)
You've always blamed me for James's death. I did all
I could do to save him. I didn't see you trying to help
him.

                    JULIAN
Shut up.

                    NANCY
Do you know what killed him, Julian?

                    JULIAN
I said shut up.

                         NANCY
Jealousy killed your brother. Ja—

He takes the straight razor out of his pocket and cuts her
throat. Julian stands at the foot of the bed as he listens to Nancy
gurgling.

INT. HOSPITAL/HALLWAY - NIGHT

Julian slowly opens the door. He steps out and casually walks
down the hallway.

                    FEMALE NURSE (O.S.)
          Excuse me, sir.

Julian stops. He doesn't turn around.

                         JULIAN
          Yes.

                    FEMALE NURSE
          Did you just come out of Mrs. Montanoro's room?

                         JULIAN
          Yes, she's sleeping.

The NURSE walks toward him.

                    FEMALE NURSE
          Only family members are allowed to visit. What's
          your name?

                         JULIAN
          Peter Clark.

Julian continues to walk down the hallway.

INT. HOSPITAL/ELEVATOR - NIGHT

The elevator arrives, and Julian enters. Another elevator door opens, and John steps out.

John sees Julian just as the elevator door closes.

INT. HOSPITAL/HALLWAY - NIGHT

John runs toward Nancy's room as he hears a commotion down the hallway. He is stopped by the Female Nurse who spotted Julian.

Two SECURITY GUARDS stand guard in front of Nancy's room.

                         JOHN
          What's going on? What's wrong with my wife? Why
          are these men here?

                      FEMALE NURSE
          I'm sorry, Mr. Montanoro. Your wife—

John pushes her out of the way and runs to the room. The guards try to stop him, but he manages to push his way into the room.

He sees Nancy lying on the bed, soaked in blood.

                    JOHN
Oh, my God!

John backs away. He grabs the Female Nurse by the arm.

                JOHN (CONTINUING)
What the hell happened?

                FEMALE NURSE
I was going to check up on her, and that's when I saw
a man walking out of her room.

                    JOHN
What man?

                FEMALE NURSE
Your height, wearing a gray trench.

                    JOHN
Was he young? Old? Did you speak to him?

John's eyes tear up.

                FEMALE NURSE
Yes, I did.

                    JOHN
What did he say?

                FEMALE NURSE
Um…Clark, Peter Clark.

John starts running down the hallway toward the elevators.

INT. KIKI'S HOME/FOYER - NIGHT

Kiki walks Adam to the front door.

> ADAM
> Hey, I'm sorry about what happened.

> KIKI
> It's not your fault. That kid is a mental case. He's nuttier than a fruitcake.

Kiki rubs her neck.

> ADAM
> I don't know what to say.

> KIKI
> Stay away from him, Adam. I'm serious. I may not be the nicest person in the world...

They both start laughing.

> KIKI (CONTINUING)
> Honey, I make no excuses for what I am, but I'm being serious. I care about you. Be careful, and stay away from him.

She opens the door, and a heavy wind blows into the house.

ADAM

The winds picked up. Are you sure you're going to be OK?

KIKI

Honey, it's nothing a good pill won't take care of. Have a good night.

ADAM

Good, I'm glad to see—

Kiki closes the door on Adam midsentence.

INT. KIKI'S HOME/FOYER - NIGHT

Kiki turns off the light and goes up the stairs.

Jason walks out of the living room holding a rope. He is wearing a black thermal mask, black gloves, and a blue sweater.

INT. KIKI'S HOME/BEDROOM - NIGHT

Kiki lies on her bed smoking a joint. She sees a set of keys on her nightstand.

She picks them up.

KIKI

Adam, you idiot. You forgot your keys.

Kiki turns on the radio and starts listening to a Depeche Mode song. She looks in her bag and pulls out a bottle of pills. She takes one out and swallows it.

> KIKI (CONTINUING)
> (to herself)
> I'm ready for that ride.

Kiki faces the window and looks out. She does not see Jason standing in the doorway.

EXT. HOSPITAL/PARKING LOT - NIGHT

The elevator doors opens, and John steps out. He runs toward his car.

INT. HOSPITAL/PARKING LOT/JOHN'S CAR - NIGHT

John sits in his car crying. He starts to bang his fists on the dashboard. He takes out his cell phone and calls Julian.

John has a puzzled look on his face as he removes the phone from his ear. There is a phone ringing inside his car.

Julian jumps up from the backseat and wraps a belt around John's neck. He presses his feet against the back of John's seat and pulls back.

INT. KIKI'S HOME/BEDROOM - NIGHT

Kiki sees Jason's reflection in the window. Before she can scream, he wraps the noose around her neck and tightens it.

She begins to struggle with him. She grabs a lamp and hits him over the head.

She starts to run with the noose wrapped around her neck, but Jason grabs the rope and pulls. Kiki jerks back and falls to the floor.

INT. HOSPITAL/PARKING LOT/JOHN'S CAR - NIGHT

Julian pulls the belt harder. John scratches the roof of the car as he gasps for air.

> JULIAN
> How does it feel? You motherfucker!

John continues to struggle as Julian pulls harder.

INT. KIKI'S HOME/BEDROOM - NIGHT

Jason throws the rope over the wooden beam and starts pulling.

INT. HOSPITAL/PARKING LOT/JOHN'S CAR - NIGHT

John's lifeless arms fall to his side. Julian lets go of the belt and sits back, breathing heavily. He takes off the trench coat and drops the open flask and the straight razor on the back seat. He gets out of the car and closes the door.

INT. KIKI'S HOME/BEDROOM - NIGHT

Jason secures the rope to the bedpost. Kiki struggles as she hangs from the wooden beam.

She reaches out to Jason and grabs him by the sweater. He pulls back as she tears off a piece.

Her eyes close, and she stops moving.

Jason takes off the thermal mask and stares at Kiki's dead body as it swings back and forth.

> ADAM (O.S.)
> What have you done?

Jason turns to Adam's voice. They stare at each other for a moment. Adam looks at Kiki's body and then back at Jason. Jason's eyes start to tear up as he moves closer to Adam.

> JASON
> I'm sorry, Adam.

Jason punches Adam in the face, knocking him down. He picks the lamp up from the floor and smashes it over Adam's head. Jason drops the lamp and kneels next to Adam's convulsing body.

> JASON (CONTINUING)
> (eyes tearing)
> I'm so sorry…I never wanted this to happen to you.

Adam stops moving. Jason gently caresses Adam's hair and kisses him on the forehead. He picks up the thermal mask and leaves the bedroom.

INT. CLARK HOME/KITCHEN - NIGHT

Amanda sits at the kitchen table typing into her laptop.

The front door suddenly bursts open, startling her, as a massive wind blows into the house.

INT. CLARK HOME/FOYER - NIGHT

Amanda closes the front door and locks it. She hears a noise coming from above her.

> AMANDA
> Adam, is that you?

INT. MONTCLAIR HIGH SCHOOL/PETER'S OFFICE - NIGHT

Peter opens the drawer and takes out the flask. He's about to drink from it when he hears the sound of his fax machine. He removes the printed papers and goes through them.

> PETER
> I knew it!

He drops the flask, and the liquor spills all over him.

> PETER (CONTINUING)
> Fuck…

He picks up the phone and calls Amanda.

> PETER (CONTINUING)
> I fucking knew it…

INT. CLARK HOME/FOYER - NIGHT

Amanda cautiously goes up the stairs. She reaches the top, and her cell phone rings.

She answers.

> AMANDA
> Hello.

INT. MONTCLAIR HIGH SCHOOL/PETER'S OFFICE -NIGHT

> PETER
> Amanda, where are you?

> AMANDA (O.S.)
> I'm home, Dad.

> PETER
> Stay there. I'm on my way.

> AMANDA (O.S.)
> Is everything OK?

> PETER
> Where's your brother?

The other phone line rings. Nathan's name flashes on the caller ID.

>   AMANDA (O.S.)
>   I think he and Jason are still at Kiki's.

>   PETER
>   What? He's with Jason?

>   AMANDA
>   Yeah, they're at Kiki's working on a class project.

>   PETER
>   Amanda, listen to me. If he gets home before I do,
>   tell him that I want him to stay put.

>   AMANDA (O.S.)
>   All right. Are you OK?

>   PETER
>   Just stay put. I'll explain everything to the both of
>   you when I get home.

>   AMANDA (O.S.)
>   OK. Oh, Dad, before I forget, Mr. Montanoro
>   dropped by.

>   PETER
>   What did he want?

AMANDA (O.S.)
He brought you over a duffel bag.

PETER
Do you know what's in it?

AMANDA (O.S.)
No. He said that you would know what to do with it.

PETER
What? Never mind that. Honey, give me Kiki's
address.

Peter places the printed papers on his desk.

It is a newspaper article that says *Mother acquitted of son's death*.
There is a picture of Nancy and her attorney in the courtroom.

EXT. KIKI'S HOME - NIGHT

Peter's car pulls up in front of Kiki's house. He gets out of the car
and starts to frantically knock on Kiki's door.

There is no answer. Peter knocks again.

PETER
Cassandra, are you there? Adam, are you there?

Peter turns the knob and opens the door. He enters the house.

INT. KIKI'S HOME/FOYER - NIGHT

It is completely dark except for the light shining down the stairway.

PETER
Adam, are you still here?

He walks up the stairs.

INT. KIKI'S HOME/BEDROOM - NIGHT

Peter slowly opens the door. He sees Kiki hanging from the beam and Adam lying in a pool of blood.

PETER
Oh, no, no...

He lifts Adam from the floor and cradles him. He closes his eyes and cries uncontrollably.

PETER (CONTINUING)
Why didn't you listen to me?

Peter gently lays Adam on the floor. He looks at himself in the mirror, only to see Adam's blood all over his shirt. We see the anger in his face as he runs out of the bedroom.

INT. CLARK HOME/STAIRWAY - NIGHT

Amanda walks down the stairs holding a duffel bag.

She stops as she sees that the front door is open.

> AMANDA
> Adam? Are you here?

There is no response. She leaves the house and closes the door behind her.

EXT. CLARK HOME - NIGHT

Amanda walks toward the Montanoro house holding the duffel bag.

She sees that there is someone looking out of Julian's bedroom window. The figure disappears, and the lights turn off.

INT. PETER'S CAR - NIGHT

Peter calls Amanda.

> AMANDA (O.S.)
> Hey, Dad.

> PETER
> Amanda, where are you?

AMANDA (O.S.)
What? I can hardly hear you. The wind's picked up.

PETER
Where are you?

AMANDA (O.S.)
(speaking loudly)
I'm going over to Julian's.

PETER
No! No! Don't go over there! Go to the police
station!

AMANDA (O.S.)
Dad, I can hardly hear you.

PETER
Meet me at the police station!

AMANDA (O.S.)
(speaking loudly)
Dad, the connection is really bad. I'm just going over
to see if Adam is there.

PETER
No! No!

AMANDA (O.S.)
(speaking loudly)
Just so you know, there was nothing in the bag. It was empty.

PETER
Don't go over there!

Amanda's signal drops.

Peter's phone rings. He sees that it is Nathan calling. Peter answers the phone and puts it on speaker.

PETER (CONTINUING)
They did it! They killed him!

NATHAN (O.S.)
Peter, calm down and tell me what happened!

PETER
Nathan, they killed him! They killed my son!

NATHAN (O.S.)
(calmly)
Peter, where are you?

PETER
I'm getting Amanda. She's headed to the Montanoro house.

NATHAN (O.S.)
No, Peter. Come to the station. We'll send a car to the Montanoro residence.

PETER
Yes, yes, send a car! I'll be there.

NATHAN (O.S.)
No, Peter. It's best that you come here.

PETER
Send a car, Nathan.

Peter hangs up.

EXT. MONTANORO HOME - NIGHT

Amanda knocks on the door, and Julian opens it.

JULIAN
Hey, what's up?

AMANDA
Hi, can I come in?

JULIAN
Sure.

INT. MONTANORO HOME/LIVING ROOM - NIGHT

Amanda and Julian sit on the sofa.

> JULIAN
> What brings you here?

Amanda looks at Julian strangely.

> AMANDA
> I was just wondering if Jason and Adam are back
> from Kiki's. I haven't heard from Adam.

> JASON (O.S.)
> Hey, Amanda, What's up?

Julian and Amanda turn to Jason. He is dressed differently.

> AMANDA
> Oh, you're back. Where's Adam?

> JASON
> He decided to stay behind.

EXT. MONTANORO HOME - NIGHT

Peter's car pulls up. He gets out of the car and opens the trunk.
He takes out a tire iron and walks toward the house.

INT. MONTANORO HOME/LIVING ROOM - NIGIIT

There is knock on the door.

> JULIAN
> I'll get it.

> AMANDA
> (to Jason)
> So, what did you guys work on?

Jason does not answer.

INT. MONTANORO HOME/FOYER - NIGHT

Julian opens the door.

Peter stands in the doorway, shaking and holding the tire iron.

> JULIAN
> What's up, Peter?

Peter does not answer. Julian looks at the tire iron and back at Peter.

> JULIAN (CONTINUING)
> (referring to the tire iron)
> Bold choice.

Peter swings the tire iron at Julian and misses him. Julian kicks Peter in the stomach, and Peter drops the weapon.

Peter rushes toward Julian, picks him up, and throws him down on the living room floor.

INT. MONTANORO HOME/LIVING ROOM - NIGHT

> AMANDA
> Dad, what's going on!

Peter punches Julian in the face over and over again. Amanda and Jason try to pull Peter off of him.

Peter grabs Jason, punches him in the face, and knocks him down.

Peter lifts Jason up, grips his shirt, and punches him in the face again.

> PETER
> (to Jason)
> You killed my son!

> AMANDA
> Dad, what are you talking about? What happened to Adam?

Julian gets up and runs into the kitchen. Peter lets go of Jason and goes after Julian.

Amanda gets in Peter's way.

AMANDA (CONTINUING)
Dad, stop it! Stop it! They didn't do anything!

PETER
They killed your brother!

He pushes Amanda out of the way.

INT. MONTANORO HOME/KITCHEN - NIGHT

Julian dials 911.

EMERGENCY OPERATOR (O.S.)
Nine one one, emergency…

Peter charges into the kitchen, grabs Julian, and bangs his head on the table. The phone falls to the floor.

JULIAN
(screaming)
Somebody, help me! He's trying to kill me!

Peter swings at Julian and misses. Julian opens one of the counter drawers and pulls out a knife. Peter knocks it out of his hand and picks it up.

AMANDA (O.S.)
Dad, drop the knife, please!

Jason charges into the kitchen and jumps on Peter. Peter elbows him in the stomach, and Jason falls to the floor.

AMANDA (CONTINUING)
Dad, please stop! You're hurting him!

Jason picks up the telephone and presses the speaker button.

EMERGENCY OPERATOR
(over the speaker phone)
There is a car heading your way...

PETER
(to Jason)
I'll fucking kill you!

He takes the phone from Jason and smashes it over his head. Peter turns his attention back to Julian.

Peter grabs Julian and throws him on the table. He holds the knife to Julian's neck.

PETER (CONTINUING)
I'm going slit your throat from ear to ear.

Julian smiles and spits blood in Peter's face. A hand grabs Peter's arm. Peter turns around, takes the knife, and stabs Amanda.

Amanda looks down at her stomach and then back up at Peter. She slowly falls to the floor with the knife still embedded in her.

PETER (CONTINUING)
(screaming)
No!

Peter falls to his knees as Julian gets off the table. Peter looks up at Julian.

> PETER (CONTINUING)
> Look what you made me do!

Amanda looks up at Julian. He looks back at her and remains silent.

She looks back at Peter, closes her eyes, and stops breathing.

> PETER (CONTINUING)
> No! Oh, my God!

> JULIAN
> She's dead. There's no use crying over her. It's not like you can bring her back.

Peter grabs one of Julian's legs, and Julian falls to the floor. Julian tries to get back up but is stopped by Peter, who is now holding another knife.

Peter gets on top of him and lifts the knife.

> JULIAN (CONTINUING)
> Go, ahead. I fucking dare you. You're a coward, Peter…an alcoholic that never amounted to anything…a poor excuse for a father and a husband…your wife and children are dead because of you.

NATHAN (O.S.)
Peter, get off of him!

Peter turns to Nathan's voice.

PETER
Nathan, I didn't do any of this.

Nathan and two POLICE OFFICERS point their revolvers at Peter.

NATHAN
Get off of him, Peter, nice and slowly.

PETER
Man, you know I couldn't do something like this.

Nathan does not respond.

PETER (CONTINUING)
Come on, man. We've been friends since we were kids. You know I couldn't do something like this.

JULIAN
(to Nathan)
Please, help me. He tried to kill us.

NATHAN
Peter, I'm not going to tell you again. Get off of him.

                    PETER
I didn't do anything.

                    NATHAN
You need help, Peter. We're going to get you some
help.

Peter looks down at Julian.

Julian has a sinister smirk on his face.

Peter looks at Nathan and then back at Julian.

                    PETER
    You fucker!

Peter brings down the knife just as Nathan's revolver goes off.
Julian moves out of the way as Peter's body lands next to him.

Nathan goes over to Julian and kicks the knife away from Peter.

                    NATHAN
It's OK. You're going to be OK.

Nathan helps Julian up, and they both look at Peter squirming
on the floor.

                    PETER
        (crying)
You have to listen to me, Nathan…You have to
listen.

Nathan turns back to Julian.

                    NATHAN
        Let's take care of you and your brother first.
                (to the officers)
        Go get the paramedics.

The two officers leave the kitchen. Julian kneels next to his brother.

                    JULIAN
        Jason, are you OK? Can you hear me?

Jason grabs Julian's hand and opens his eyes. Nathan helps him up.

                    NATHAN
                (to Jason)
        Are you OK?

                    JASON
        I'm fine.

Jason looks over to Peter.

                    JASON (CONTINUING)
        Is he dead?

                    JULIAN
        No.
                (to Nathan)
        He killed Amanda. I saw him stab her.

                    JASON
Where's my dad? I want my dad.

                    NATHAN
Look, the both of you will be fine. The paramedics
are right outside.

Julian and Jason walk out of the kitchen. Nathan stays behind
and goes over to Peter. He looks at Amanda's body and then at
Peter.

He takes out his handcuffs, kneels down, and cuffs Peter.

              NATHAN (CONTINUING)
        (to Peter)
What did you do, man?

He looks back to Julian and Jason as both brothers exit the house.
Two PARAMEDICS enter the kitchen and head toward Nathan.

              NATHAN (CONTINUING)
We've got one dead and one wounded.

Nathan gets up as the paramedics lift Peter and place him on a
gurney. He leaves the kitchen.

MONTAGE:

EXT. MONTANORO HOME/STREET - NIGHT

A POLICE OFFICER keeps a crowd of people at bay.

The paramedics wheel Peter out of the house. He screams and struggles maniacally as he is wheeled past Julian and Jason.

Amanda's body is wheeled out of the house in a body bag.

INT. HOSPITAL/NANCY'S ROOM - NIGHT

POLICE OFFICERS enter Nancy's room as a nurse covers her face with a white sheet.

INT. HOSPITAL/PARKING LOT/JOHN'S CAR - NIGHT

POLICE OFFICERS pull John's body out of the car.

They find Peter's gray trench, straight razor, and his flask.

INT. KIKI'S HOME/BEDROOM - NIGHT

PARAMEDICS place Kiki in a body bag.

A POLICE OFFICER takes the torn piece of the blue sweater and places it into an evidence bag.

INT. CLARK HOME/PETER'S BEDROOM - NIGHT

Nathan is in Peter's bedroom.

An OFFICER finds the ripped blue sweater.

Another OFFICER finds two pieces of a baseball bat and hands them to Nathan.

INT. MONTANORO HOME/LIVING ROOM - NIGHT

Julian throws the remaining pieces of the second baseball bat into the fire. He looks at his brother suspiciously.

Jason turns and walks out of the living room with a sinister smirk on his face.

INT. MENTAL INSTITUTION - DAY

Peter is in a white padded room.

He is strapped to his bed. He laughs uncontrollably as he struggles with the straps.

INT. JULIAN'S CAR - DAY

Julian is driving down New York's west side highway. Jason is holding his iPhone and staring at a picture of Adam.

Julian takes the iPhone away from him and deletes the picture of Adam.

He hands the iPhone back to Jason.

EXT. **PRESENT DAY**/NEW YORK CITY STREET - DAY

The city streets are crowded with people walking in all directions.

From the distance we see the twin brothers, now in their early thirties, walking down the street.

Julian is wearing a fitted suit and holding a briefcase. Jason is dressed casually. He wears a shirt that shows off his muscular physique. They both smile in confidence as they continue to walk down the street.

FADE OUT.

32230038R00110

Made in the USA
Lexington, KY
12 May 2014